Recreating
Brief
Therapy
Preferences and Possibilities

By the same authors

Becoming Solution-focused in Brief Therapy

A NORTON PROFESSIONAL BOOK

Recreating
Brief
Therapy

Preferences and Possibilities

JOHN L. WALTER

JANE E. PELLER

W. W. Norton & Company
New York · London

For information about permission to reproduce selections
from this book, write to
Permissions, W.W. Norton & Company, Inc., 500 Fifth Avenue,
New York, NY 10110

Composition by Ken Gross
Manufacturing by Haddon Craftsmen

Library of Congress Cataloging-in-Publication Data
Walter, John L., 1945–
 Recreating brief therapy : preferences and possibilities / John L. Walter,
Jane E. Peller.
  p. cm.
 "A Norton professional book."
 Includes bibliographical references and index.
 ISBN 0-393-70325-8
 1. Brief therapy. 2. Psychotherapy. I. Peller, Jane E. II. Title.

RC480.5.W276 2000
616.89'14 — dc21 00-020986

W.W. Norton & Company, Inc., 500 Fifth Avenue, New York, NY 10110
www.wwnorton.com
W.W. Norton & Company Ltd., 10 Coptic Street, London WC1A 1PU

1 2 3 4 5 6 7 8 9 0

To Nate

Acknowledgments

This book was inspired by many conversations, including those with our clients, with participants in workshops, with friends and colleagues, with authors through the books we have read, and with readers of our manuscript at various stages of development. Thus, this book has had many coauthors. While some will remain anonymous, we would like to thank those we can.

First, we want to thank all those readers of our first book who said, "This is the best book on solution-focused brief therapy. When is the next one coming out?" Your feedback inspired us to continue working and writing.

We would like to thank our readers of various parts and stages of this manuscript for their generous reading, encouragement, and suggestions. They include Peggy Solow Liss, Jerry Gale, and Lois Shawver.

We want to thank Gene Combs and Jill Freedman for reading some of the early chapters and providing affirmation and exchange about some of our postmodern ideas. Conversations with them inspired us to be sensitive to social justice and the power within diversity.

We would like to thank our friend Michael Banks, not just for his reading of the entire manuscript but for his generously offering us encouragement as well as some of his ideas and metaphors from his notions of conversational change.

Our thanks as well goes to our friend and colleague Scott Miller. Conversations with him as we collaborated on our intensive trainings have inspired some ideas and demystified others. A fellow writer and developer of ideas, he shared his experience in a way that was affirming and heartening.

We would also like to thank Jane's father, Bert Peller. His reading of the manuscript left us feeling that we were not alone. We felt we had someone else who worried along with us (perhaps also lost some sleep) and struggled to find clearer and more coherent ways to express our ideas.

We would also like to thank those who gave us their support for our ideas, namely, Jim Duvall, Gaby Mueller-Moskau, Gerd Mueller, Rudi Kronbichler, Eve Lipchik, Jennifer Andrews and David Clark.

Finally, we would like to thank our Norton editors, Susan Munro and Deborah Malmud, who pushed for clarity and kept us on schedule.

Contents

Introduction

Starting with Desire

This book began as an attempt to summarize and describe our advances in brief therapy. As we began to think about that goal we realized that our work had progressed beyond what we initially considered. In fact, we had been restless for quite some time about limitations of our practices. We felt cramped by the traditional focuses on problems and solutions. We felt restricted by linear interpretations that were at the heart of traditional goal- and outcome- oriented approaches. We were concerned that in our zeal to be positively oriented we were not listening sufficiently to our clients.

While these concerns were coming increasingly to the fore over a period of years, we also were reading a number of social scientists, practitioners, and philosophers who collectively would be described as postmodern, poststructural, postpositivist, pragmatic, feminist, or narrative. From our reading of some postmodern thinking, we adopted the key distinction of *desire* as our starting point and from there began to ask ourselves some different questions. If we adopt the idea that there are differences in people's desires and we assume that people participate in different ways of desiring, knowing, and acting, then several questions arise: "How can we respect and coordinate our actions with many diverse and different people?" "How can we create narratives that make meaning of our lives?" "How do we want our personal and public worlds to be?" and "How might we approach our clients and their desires differently?"

As we considered these questions, we realized that we had moved fully into new metaphors. This amounted to a recontextualization or a recreation of how we go about our work. Our former language no longer served to describe our work. To describe or recreate brief therapy within new metaphors, we needed to construct a new vocabulary. This book is a call for a new language, a language beyond "therapy" and the discourses of pathology and deficits. At the same time it suggests a language to answer that call.

We begin by describing in the first chapter our own professional changes over the past 18 years as we shifted from a treatment orientation to new language and orientation we call *personal consultation.** This shift was profound for us, as we moved away from the language of pathology and assessment to an orientation toward and vocabulary of conversation, personal consultation, possibilities, and optimism. It has led to our thinking of our clients as customers of a consulting service—and this has made us more sensitive to client desires, more optimistic about change, and closer to clients emotionally and pragmatically.

In chapter one, we trace our changes through several orientations and models in order to provide you with an understanding of where we have come from as well as how we decided to work as we now do. This story of our development provides a context for later chapters.

In chapter two, we widen the scope of our change by locating it within several shifts from modernism to postmodernism within philosophy, humanities, and social sciences. We describe five shifts that have direct bearing on helping clients and discuss how they make a difference in thinking and practice. These ideas not only take us out of discourses of pathology and deficit but help us to recreate our work in terms of client desire and preferences. We find that this vocabulary allows us to see our clients as well intentioned people who want to create something positive in their future. It also allows us to see ourselves as standing alongside our clients as they seek out and create these preferred futures. This preference orientation seems a more useful fit for a contemporary era of diversity and plurality.

As a consequence of these shifts in thinking, our basic research question changed from, *"How do we construct solutions?"* to *"How can we create a space of dialogue and wonder where purpose, preferences, and possibilities can emerge and evolve?"* The remainder of this book is our current response to this question.

Many books begin with a list of assumptions that guide the work, but we found such a list to be too confining and suggestive of a defined practice. Instead, in chapter three we create a tentative list of *inquiries* to highlight that what we are presenting is not a model or packaged way of working but

---

*Throughout this book, we will refer to our work as "personal consultation" and to ourselves as consultants, rather than therapists. We first published our use of this term in *Becoming Solution-focused in Brief Therapy* in 1992, and later in both *The Handbook of Solution-focused Brief Therapy* (1996), edited by Miller, Hubble, and Duncan, and *Paradigms of Clinical Social Work, Volume 2* (1998), edited by Rachelle Dorfman. We use the term *personal consultation* because it more accurately reflects the desire orientation and non-pathology orientation of our work. When referring to other orientations, we will use the word *therapy*.

an inquiry into creativity. Throughout this book we share our inquiries into possible ways of working and different conversations with our clients.

Chapter four introduces the conversational metaphor and the consultant disposition of being "curious with" the client. The conversational metaphor sets up a nonhierarchical relationship where the consultant facilitates an open space in which clients can speak of their concerns, their desires, and their successes. The consultant adopts a disposition of both curiosity and wonder with clients about their emerging preferences and purposes.

Chapter five invites the reader to step beyond traditional thinking of problem/solution to consider an orientation to client preferences and possibilities. This approach is about pursuing client wants but with a postmodern twist. Rather than defining goals in a specific and behavioral fashion, we choose the word *preferences* and define it in terms of conversational processes. Thus, this chapter describes purpose as arising from within the conversation and speaks of these conversations as *preferencing*.

Chapter six discusses how conversations can be opened further by conversing about the significance of change. Overly focused language can be opened up by conceptualizing the client's initially stated preferences as a means to something else, which often has a broader and more open meaning.

Chapter seven talks about "sign" language and embraces the metaphors of brainstorming and visualization, which break us out of the linear thinking of traditional action-oriented models. Talking with clients about what would be the signs to them that things were going more the way they want introduces preferences, possibilities, and optimism.

Chapter eight discusses the inquiry of difference or success. The emphasis here is on how to be sensitive to and how to amplify stories of success in terms of self-agency.

Consistent with our conversational metaphor is the idea of inviting other voices into the conversation. Chapter nine shows how to do this and discusses how the reflections of others can not only bring out the power of different opinions or possibilities but also contribute to an open atmosphere within the conversation.

The metaphor of conversation includes reflections on what has been said. Using examples of reflecting and encouraging conversations, chapter ten illustrates our reflecting and encouraging dispositions.

Chapter eleven provides one story of a complete consultation. We follow the dialogue, as well as other changes that took place, over several meetings with a client, demonstrating how the conversation evolves and how a personal consultation comes to an end.

Recreating
Brief
Therapy
Preferences and Possibilities

CHAPTER ONE

A Rewarding Professional Change

From Therapy to Personal Consultation

Recently we saw a client for several meetings. The client described a horrible life situation. As a child she had been abused by her father. She had gone through one divorce, and now she was having great difficulty with her second husband. Her financial situation had deteriorated because her unemployed husband had not paid the bills, and she was drinking rather heavily just to cope with all the problems. She had been hospitalized once for her drinking, had relapsed, been hospitalized and released again.

As we reviewed videotapes of the meetings with the client, we experienced a number of reactions. We were surprised by how different these reactions were from what we think they might have been if we had seen this client several years earlier. If we had seen this client several years earlier, we would have been overwhelmingly impressed by the difficulties and tragedies of this woman's situation. We not only would have felt bad for her, but also would have felt mostly the hopelessness that she was expressing.

Now we were impressed not with just the extreme difficulty that we would have heard before, but also with the heart and courage of this woman. Even while telling us of the tragedies of her life, she was saying how she was continuing to "hang in there." She was still keeping hope alive and trying to make things better for herself and for her kids. How was it that we were hearing her courage rather than just the difficulty that we would have heard before? How could it be that we were optimistic for her?

At the end of her meetings with us, the client expressed these reactions.

CLIENT: This has been very helpful.
PERSONAL CONSULTANT: Anything specific that was helpful?
CLIENT: When I first came over here, I was depressed and I thought I could

rely on you, and open up to you, and that I could tell you things. Other people I have gone to, I did not feel comfortable with.

CONSULTANT: Anything I did or didn't do that made you feel that way?

CLIENT: No, your confidence in me really helped me a lot.

CONSULTANT: My confidence in you?

CLIENT: Yes, your confidence pushed me a lot to have confidence in myself. The first time I came here I had said to myself, "I'm not going to make it." But I did.

CONSULTANT: Yes, you did, you really did.

Client stories like this have inspired us to reflect on how come we hear clients' stories differently. How is it that this client felt that we had confidence in her? We had not deliberately decided to convince her that we had confidence in her. How is it that we are hearing courage where before we might have heard only the overwhelming circumstances? How is it that clients are hearing our reflections of them differently? Could our current orientation be contributing to this different listening?

We wondered, too, how come we feel more emotionally touched now by what clients are telling us and by what is happening in our meetings with clients. In some ways we feel more drawn to what people are telling us. In other ways, we feel more moved by what is happening within the meeting. Could it be that people are different in the meeting with us? Are we different with our clients? How so?

Pondering these changes, we have reflected increasingly on the way we work and on how we might describe this new way of working. Several stories could account for these changes, but the central one for us centers on a shift in language from "therapy" to "personal consultation." This shift characterizes the move from a discourse of interview, strategy, and intervention to one of conversation, curiosity, reflection, and encouragement. It marks a major change in worldview and practice. Since this shift did not occur all at once, we would like to share with you the story of our evolution to this point.

SITUATING OUR PROFESSIONAL CHANGE

From Clients as Patients to Clients as Customers

Back in late seventies, we were both involved in intrapsychic paradigms that focused either on deficiencies in internal dynamics or on biological explanations for problems. In our different ways we both became frustrated and concerned with the slow rate of change in our clients despite our growth-oriented practices and with the pessimism that diagnostic categorizing seemed to project. At the same time, we were both involved in family therapy approaches based on systems theories. Pursuing these theories, we learned about roles within families, scapegoating, and how structural deficiencies within these systems appeared to be the cause of problems within families.

Both of these orientations, intrapsychic and systemic, taught us to appreciate the tragedy and suffering of the people we saw. Each orientation had its advantages. The intrapsychic orientation made us appreciate the internal struggles of each client. The systems orientation gave us a contextual and interactional view. Attempting to think in terms of both individual and family structures at the same time, however, left us muddled. We recall being involved in disposition staffings at that time and being confused by the arguments taking place between staff representing different paradigms. Those of the intrapsychic persuasion would argue how the depression of a client, who was a father, resulted from a history of passive dependence that probably began in early childhood. They would argue for a long-term growth therapy to treat the characterological problems of his reacting passive-dependently to the circumstances of his life. Those representing the family systems paradigm would argue that the father's depression resulted from his changed role and loss of importance in the family, now that his children had left home and his wife had taken on a job outside of the home for the first time. They would argue for family sessions to help the husband and wife make needed adjustments in their roles and expectations. Often, the disposition resulted in a compromise, with a recommendation for both types of therapy at the same time.

The problem for us was not in the usefulness of either one of these orientations, but the challenge of making sense of both of them at the same time, across the logical levels of intrapsychic and interactional. If both were claiming explanatory power, could both be true even when they seemed mutually exclusive? If we argued that only one orientation could be true, what did that mean about the other? We found that our attempts to integrate the intrapsychic and systemic paradigms only left us more confused—until we realized that we were attempting to integrate orientations across logical levels (Walter, 1989).

What was common to both orientations, intrapsychic and systemic, was the belief that there was an identified unit or structure to be treated.* The intrapsychic orientation chose the individual mind to treat; the family systems orientation chose the family as the unit to treat. While each of these orientations had predominance within the field and significant success as explanatory theories, we found their attempts at exclusivity to be restrictive and attempted integrations to be impossible across theoretical lines.

---

*We are using the terms *structure* and *structural* to refer in a broad sense to an essentially defined, bounded, and centered object. Structure in this sense will be contrasted with the terms nonstructured and poststructural in following chapter. Our use of these terms is not to be confused with the more specific reference to a model of therapy called structural family therapy developed by Salvador Minuchin (1978). That model is one specific instance in which treatment was directed at an identified structure, the family.

During the late seventies and early eighties, we became familiar with the work of Milton Erickson (1901-1980) and several of his followers. Their work contributed greatly to our thinking and practice. Ericksonian approaches all seemed to stress a consumer and customer orientation. Jay Haley, one of the founders of a strategic orientation, used the concept of "customer" and talked of how the therapist should be more active and directive, *strategic*, in helping clients get what they wanted (Haley, 1976, 1980). The neuro-linguistic programmers, Richard Bandler and John Grinder (1979), spoke of the need to begin therapy with the question, "What do you want?" The strength of their customer orientation strengthened our position that clients were not passive respondents to goals as determined by experts but rather customers responsible for setting the agenda.

These Ericksonian approaches also strongly emphasized both searching for client resources and utilizing them. Erickson and his followers conceptualized resources not just as assets in the environment but also as skills possessed by the individual or family. While our social work training had prepared us to look for client strengths, Ericksonian approaches took this one step further by showing how client resources could be used to solve problems or achieve goals. Our impression of pathology-oriented approaches had been that looking for client strengths was just part of the overall process in making an accurate diagnosis. Erickson and Ericksonians, in contrast, used resources directly to further change. For example, if a client were assertive with her or his boss, that skill or resource could be used in the problem context to effect change.

Overall, Erickson and his followers made us aware that there were alternatives to intrapsychic and systemic approaches that were more respectful of client initiative and client responsibility as a customer. The resulting therapy was optimistic because of its grounding in client resources. However, these approaches were still limited because they conceptualized resources as concrete entities or states. By thinking of a resource as a state, these Ericksonian approaches continued conceptualizing problems, goals, resources, skills, and solutions as entities in themselves or as properties of structural states. For example, these Ericksonian approaches would assume that a client was rather shy and dependent. The qualities would be conceptualized as deficits of the client's structural state, as if shyness and dependence were deficits or abnormalities in the client's present state. Therefore, these approaches assumed that other concrete qualities needed to be added, more confidence or self-esteem to fill in the deficits of the person. Confidence and self-esteem were labels for resources as entities.

We next involved ourselves in the brief strategic therapy model, the brief problem-focused therapy model of the Mental Research Instititute (MRI) (Weakland, Fisch, Watzlawick, & Bodin, 1974). This was the first approach within our experience to address problems in commonsense or noninterpretive language. Problems were described not in a causal fashion but merely as mistaken definitions and attempted solutions. We found this approach refreshing, because the approach did not blame anyone for problems or state that there was anything structurally wrong with anyone for having a problem. The assumption of this approach was that the way clients attempted to solve their problem was keeping the problem going or that the attempted solution was becoming a problem in itself.

For example, when a mother came in to see us and complained of her teenage daughter's increasing insolence, talking back, disobedience around home chores, and not attending church, we heard her interpretation of her daughter's conduct as bad behavior. As the mother interpreted her daughter's conduct as bad, she attempted to solve the problem of bad behavior through punishment. The girl was now grounded for the next several months, and in order to monitor the grounding mother had to stay home. This definition of the problem also meant to mother that if the daughter was bad, she was a bad mother. In shame, desperation, and fear of being a bad mother, the mother had escalated the groundings. In brief strategic terms, we mapped the pattern as one of mother escalating the punishment, only to have her daughter escalate the behavior in order to show her mother that as a teen she was independent and not about to be dominated by her mother through punishment. Mother's and daughter's ways of attempting to solve the problem as each of them defined it was keeping the problem going and contributing to the escalation of conflict.

With the brief strategic approach problems could be solved easily and quickly by assisting clients to new, reframed, and more workable definitions of their situations or perhaps to different solutions. Rather than framing the reasons for a problem in structural abnormalities and assuming that structural change or treatment was required, the brief strategic model assumed the client was a competent customer and sought to help this customer solve the problem that s/he had presented. This model accepted the client's definition of the problem, accepted what the client said about her or his situation, and accepted what the client wanted from therapy. This was a refreshing difference from structural and pathology-based approaches that assumed that the basis for a problem was some deficiency in a structural unit, such as a person, family, or couple. In this approach the problem was the problem, not a structural abnormality.

Both Ericksonian approaches and the brief strategic model oriented us to thinking about the people we saw as clients (or customers) rather than as patients. Some may think this difference is just semantic or sociological. "Patient" is a term used by medical professionals; "client" is used by non-medical professionals; "customer" is used in sales and business. Yet for us, this shift reflected a shift from structural thinking and treatment to providing a problem-solving service or *consulting*. We think this shift in language was the beginning of a much greater shift in our point of view.

As a result of our involvement with the brief strategic model, we learned a different way to define the client system. With structural approaches we had assumed that the client system was whatever system the problem was embedded in. Marital problems, therefore, required marital therapy; the client system was defined as the couple. Family problems required family therapy, and the client system was the family unit.

However, in the brief strategic model, the client system was defined not by sociological units but within language. In other words, the client system was composed of any and all who stated a belief in the problem's existence as well as a desire for the problem to be solved.

This change allowed us to see that the notion of customer could be used quite literally. Customer was not used just to indicate who within the treatment unit was most interested in change but to redefine the client system across sociological boundaries. The client or customer system was defined as *whoever wanted change*. The client system could be just one member of a troubled relationship. It could be a parent, probation officer, and teacher, all concerned about a child who may or may not be concerned about a problem. The fact that a parent, probation officer, and teacher are all concerned about a problem and willing to work with a therapist makes them all members of a client system. If the child that the parent, probation officer, and teacher are concerned about thinks there is not a problem and is not interested in change, this child is not defined as part of the client system.

However, the brief strategic model still separated the therapist from the client system and still identified the client system as bounded by the definition of the problem. The membership of the client system was defined as all those who stated there was a problem and expressed a desire to change it. In other words, the client system was defined in terms of a steady state of the problem, with someone like a therapist needed to initiate change. Since the therapist was identified as the change agent, there was a boundary drawn between therapist and client system, whereby the therapist needed to be strategic by reframing, giving directives, or posing counterparadoxes in order to initiate change. Defining the clients in terms of the steady state of a problem and the therapist as a change agent set up an opposition between the two systems (de Shazer, 1985).

From Problems to Optimism

During our early involvement in the development of the solution-focused brief therapy approach, we were in transition. While working with the Milwaukee Group (Steve de Shazer, Insoo Kim Berg, Eve Lipchik, Elam Nunnally, James Dirks, Marilyn LaCourt, Alex Molnar, Wallace Gingerich, James Wilks, and Michelle Weiner-Davis) at the Brief Family Therapy Center in the early eighties, we began to recognize that there were times when what the client had stated as the problem did not happen. These non-problem times were referred to by the Milwaukee Group as *exceptions* to the interactional pattern of the problem and the attempted solution (de Shazer,

1985). As part of this group we also began to notice that many clients reported changes before the first therapy session. These changes before the first session were called pretreatment changes (Weiner-Davis, de Shazer, & Gingerich, 1987). Thinking in terms of *exceptions to the problem* and *pretreatment change* began to poke holes in our picture of problems and their attempted solutions as stable interactional patterns. We began to wonder which was more real: the problem and attempted solution pattern or the exception and pretreatment change patterns. As we weighed the frequency of problem patterns versus exception patterns, we asked, even more radically, how useful it was to interpret clients' experiences as stable patterns. Perhaps the notion of stable patterns was just a construct that was limiting our ability to observe change. Perhaps it would be more productive to think of change as constant and randomness of behavior as the norm, rather than enduring interactional patterns as the norm. We began to think that the assumption "change is occurring all the time" might be a more useful starting point than "behavior is constant and repetitious."

Until then we had focused on a more positive direction in our work by thinking of exceptions to problems and the possibility of pretreatment change, and we were still thinking of these positives within the notion of stable interactional patterns. In other words, successful client behaviors were defined as exceptions to a problem rather than as unique or standing on their own as useful. We were still conceptualizing problems, exceptions, solutions, and goals in terms of interactional patterns.

Two more changes initiated by the Milwaukee Group took us even further from a structural way of thinking and toward a more positive or optimistic direction. The *formula first session task*, the primary task in every first session, proposed that solutions could be created without any knowledge about the problem. This task, given to almost every client at the end of the first session, went like this:

> Between now and the next time that you come in, we would like you to notice what is going on in your life (marriage, family, etc.) that you would like to see continue. (de Shazer & Molnar, 1984, p. 298)

The result of this task was that the majority of clients came back to the second session reporting change or successes since the first session.

Clients often reported change without our knowing anything about the problem. The effectiveness of this task in initiating change shook our conviction in interactional patterns and diagnostic thinking to its core. Before this we had assumed, like so many others, that we needed to know information about the problem and the interactional pattern around that problem in order to figure out what to do about the problem. We assumed that differentiation of the problem determined the therapeutic intervention or solution. For example, if someone reported problems with obsession, we assumed that we had to intervene around the belief or fear that maintained the problem. Or if someone reported constant conflicts with their spouse, we assumed we needed either to break the client's belief about needing to be right and perhaps to prescribe fighting in a paradoxical fashion to interrupt the pattern. In other words, we believed that *the nature of the problem determined what interventions were needed.*

With the results of this formula first session task, we learned that *we could help people toward positive change without ever knowing what the problem was.* We formed a new assumption—*that there was no necessary connection between the problem and the construction of a solution.* If change could be accomplished without knowing ahead of time what the problem was, *problem determination was not necessary.*

Another marker of this development of a *solution only* focus was the miracle question, which went like this:

> Suppose that one night, while you were asleep, there was a miracle and this problem was solved. How would you know? What would be different? (de Shazer, 1988, p. 5)

This question and the ensuing discussion focused clients on a future when the problem was solved. Consistent with the assumption that problem information was not necessary, the miracle question furthered the idea that what was helpful was focusing on the future telltale criteria to the client that the problem was solved and therapy was successful.

In 1986 de Shazer and his colleagues articulated this solution-focused brief therapy approach in "Brief therapy: Focused solution-development" in *Family Process.* While working within this positive and optimistic approach, we found that attempting to map client reports in terms of stable interactional patterns was becoming quite cumbersome and unnecessary.

In the mid-to-late eighties, we had moved from a treatment orientation to a consultative one. We had also moved from a problem focus to a solution focus and to an optimistic orientation. However, there was still a distance conceptually, pragmatically, and emotionally between our clients and us.

FROM OBSERVATION TO CONVERSATION

We began our 1992 book, *Becoming Solution-focused in Brief Therapy*, with the proposition that the history of psychotherapy could be summarized as attempted solutions to problems in helping people. Observing that professionals over the years struggled with how to be more helpful, or how to get unstuck from what they perceived as problems in how to be helpful, we suggested that these problems and stuck points could be stated as research questions that professionals were asking themselves. The answers professionals developed became models or orientations to therapy.

Let us revisit that historical presentation of questions and answers to set the background for the more recent changes we advocate in the remainder of this book. Each research question has certain assumptions embedded within it and these assumptions are situated in cultural and temporal circumstances. In other words, the language of the question, the assumptions within the question, and even the answers are already mediated by the beliefs within the community of inquirers.

First, we suggested that the history of psychotherapy from early in the century to around 1950 could be seen as attempts to answer the research question:

What is the cause of the problem or disorder?

The culture of psychotherapy in the early part of the century was influenced by the predominant philosophy of science at the time, called modern thinking. This question was consistent with a belief in objective science and linear, instrumental notions of causality. As we deconstructed this question, we saw that the question already predetermined a whole class of answers, that is, a class of causes. Answers to the question seemed to be within these traditional assumptions:

- Problems are what therapy is about.
- There are causes to those problems.
- Determining the cause of the problem would be helpful or necessary in order to solve the problem or cure the disorder.

This way of thinking, that there are causes to personal and emotional problems, has been so pervasive that such thinking is usually accepted as common sense. Answers have ranged, for example, from the early lack of bonding between mother and child, to genetic predispositions, to chemical imbalances, to the social environment, to personality disturbances, and so on. These answers then became more fully developed as therapy models or orientations to problem-solving. If the cause of the problem were considered to be deficiencies in early bonding, the therapy would be a long-term attempt to correct or replace that deficit in bonding. If the cause were thought to be biological, then medications or surgery might be the solution.

The predominant theories of the time were generally based on notions of efficient causality, that is, the notion that cause precedes effect. Therefore, asking "What is the cause of the problem or disorder?" already assumes that the answer will be found in the past. The scientific culture of the time also assumed that determination of the cause of any problem was necessary before the problem could be solved.

Second, we looked at a research question that began to be asked around 1950 and that led to a different class of answers:

What maintains the problem?

Out of this question arose all of the here-and-now therapy models of the '50s, '60s, and '70s, as well as all of the family systems therapy approaches. This question assumed:

- that problems were what therapy was all about,
- that problems were maintained, or kept going, by something in the present, and
- that problem maintenance implied something in the present that was ongoing as opposed to the notion of cause, which implied something in the past.

Some answered this question—What maintains the problem?—by saying that problems are maintained by irrational or faulty thinking. This answer became the centerpiece for the whole cognitive or cognitive-behavioral orientation (Beck, 1976; Ellis, 1962). Other professionals answered this question by assuming problems were maintained by interactional patterns within families. Family therapists began to use the thinking of information processing systems or first-order cybernetics in order to articulate their formulations of problem maintenance. The brief strategic therapy approach (Weakland, Fisch, Watzlawick, & Bodin, 1974), the strategic family therapy approach (Haley, 1976, 1980; Madanes, 1981), the structural family therapy approach (Minuchin, 1978), and the Milan systemic approach (Selvini-Palazzoli, Boscolo, Cecchin, & Prata, 1978) all mapped out problems in a family context and/or in terms of interactional patterns.

For all these clinicians and theorists, both of these questions, "What is the cause of the problem?" and "What maintains the problem?" assumed a structural view. The hidden assumption being made within both of these questions was that we as therapists or researchers could be objective observers of the structures of our clients and the structure of the problems. The difference between the first and second question represented a shift from one structure to a different, larger one. The unit of analysis shifted from psychic structures over to family structures. What remained the same was the assumption that we as therapists or researchers could determine objectively the answers to these questions about client systems. Both questions and answers were part of a tradition of modern science and structuralism with roots in the Enlightenment that assumed objective observation.

The next research question was:

What is the process of change?

This question, arising in the 1970s, made some very different assumptions. It assumed:

- change is what therapy is all about,
- there is a process of change, and
- the process could be identified and described.

Speer (1970) was among the first to question how useful it was to use constructs like "homeostasis" or "personality," words that described sameness and repetition in professions dedicated to change. Watzlawick, Weakland, and Fisch (1974) proposed notions of reframe and counterparadox to describe therapeutic change, claiming that if problems were described as stable patterns that were paradoxical in nature, then a counterparadox was necessary to break people out of these patterns. This process of change, however, was still conceptualized as an intervention to move clients from one stable interactional pattern surrounding the problem to a new future state that in turn would be stable. Change was posed in opposition to stability and as an exception to the more natural order of homeostasis and sameness. Of the two concepts, stability and change, stability was privileged as natural. The reversal of this privileging would have been to think of change as happening most of the time with stability as the exception.

In the eighties, as many of us in the field became fascinated with work of Milton Erickson, we began to ask another research question:

How do we construct solutions?

Erickson had not seemed too concerned with either the origins of the problem or its maintenance; instead he focused on solutions and what people wanted. This inspired us, as we watched and listened to tapes of his sessions, to ask: *How do Milton Erickson and his clients construct solutions?*

This question represented a shift of focus from problems to solutions—and away from observation of stable structures containing the problem toward observation of change. As we deconstructed it, we found these implicit assumptions:

- There was going to be a shift of focus to solutions and away from problems.
- Solutions were constructible.
- Solution construction was a joint enterprise of the therapist and client as exemplified by the pronoun "we."
- The interrogative "how" suggested there was a describable process of constructing solutions.

The assumption that solutions were constructible implied that solutions might be variable, that solutions might not be tied to causes of problems, or to the maintenance of problems, or to the categorization of particular problems.

As we discussed earlier, one of the assumptions of early solution-focused work was that *problem information was not necessary for solution construction.* Early research and discussions indicated that therapist and client need only focus on solution construction and that diagnosis of problems was not necessary (de Shazer, 1988). "How do we construct solutions?" led to our early formulations of a solution-focused approach in the early eighties.

These were still based on many of the assumptions of a problem maintenance paradigm but with a positive focus.

By the time the solution-only focus became formalized by de Shazer and the Milwaukee Group in 1986, we had moved with them away from thinking of solution-focused work as the positive flip side of problem-focused work. We were no longer thinking of times when the problem did not occur and pretreatment change as just anomalies within the brief strategic model. Our basic assumption had become that *solution development processes were independent of problem processes.* Discussing a future when the problem was solved or times when the problem did not happen produced solutions.

In 1992, as our manual on how to become solution focused was published, we realized that we were in transition. Since that time several concerns about our work have become clearer and other influences have raised more issues and inspired further advances.

Let us go back for a moment to our fundamental research question, "How do we construct solutions?" As we presented this question in workshops, participants pointed out to us that the word *solution* implied its opposite—the word *problem*. While we were working in a solution-focused fashion, our word, solution, suggested that we still believed in a problem/ solution distinction. We began to wonder about the possible limits of our staying within that configuration. How might we still be connecting ourselves to problem/solution baggage? Were we merely privileging the positive side of the problem/solution distinction? Certainly there were advantages to focusing on the solution side after decades of pathology and problem-solving models; however, we became concerned that we were just substituting one focus for the other while remaining within the language of observable processes. Was there something to be gained by abandoning this notion of observable and predictable processes altogether? Perhaps there was more to be gained by abandoning the problem/solution distinction, the notion of interactional patterns, and the notion of observable processes.

To describe our sessions as solution construction inevitably linked our thinking to notions of problem maintenance. Additionally, many of our client meetings did not seem to follow "a" process or solution-focused decision tree (de Shazer, 1988; Walter & Peller, 1992). We needed a different way of thinking to eliminate the feeling of being confined by the problem/solution distinction and to make better sense of the fact that our sessions did not seem to follow a predicted process.

We also became concerned about the possible limitations of the verb "do" in "How *do* we construct solutions?" Were we limiting ourselves to present-time descriptions of what we thought we were doing? Might there not be more useful questions for us to ask ourselves about our work? Also, by focusing on what we do and on descriptions, is it fair to say that all sessions should or do go that way?

We also became concerned about our concretized notion of goals. Within the Ericksonian tradition, we had included goals as part of solution construction. We insisted that the goals of therapy had to be well-defined and we developed a list of criteria for well-defined goals. Goals had to be:

1. positively defined (as the presence of something rather than the absence),
2. process or action-oriented,
3. in the here and now,
4. specific and preferably in behavioral or concrete terms,
5. within the client's control, and
6. within the client's language.

We realized, however, that attempting to have clients define their goals specifically and in such a targeted fashion was also difficult and possibly confining. When we followed our agenda of getting well-defined goals, clients often felt misheard or not heard. In workshops, we found that participants became overly focused on the criteria, as if they were rules that superseded listening to the client and maintaining rapport.

We also found that initial goal statements by clients were often vague and that the language changed over time. Yet some clients still achieved what they wanted even when the goals never became specifically defined. For other clients, the language of their goals changed from one session to the next. These clients also achieved what they wanted without our having to pin their goals down with the criteria.

So, where had this assumption that goals had to be specified and/or well-defined come from? We had adopted the need for goals to be well-specified from the tradition of problem-solving and goal-achieving orientations, for example, brief problem-focused therapy (Weakland, Fisch, Watzlawick, & Bodin, 1974) and neuro-linguistic programming (Bandler & Grinder, 1979), among others. In this tradition, the overarching assumption is that clients have to *do something* or *do something different* in order for change to happen. The logic was that, since client action was necessary in order to solve a problem or achieve a goal, then having the goal or action well-specified was necessary. Specificity made the action more manageable in the client's eyes and more measurable in both the client's and therapist's eyes. The focus then became on defining client action, motivating the client to take the action, and determining what it meant about the client if s/he did not. However, we found that client action was not always necessary. So, we began to wonder about our continuing to assume that client action was necessary and that goals had to be well specified.

Overall, we became concerned that in our zeal to be solution-focused we had perhaps overemphasized the technology of constructing solutions and underemphasized the human part of interacting with our clients. Perhaps we were becoming solution-*forced*, as some were beginning to warn (Nylund & Corsiglia, 1994).

Meanwhile, we found that our transition away from structural thinking was not a smooth or easy one. We were concerned about the baggage we were carrying with us from structural thinking and the consequences of thinking that we as therapist-researchers could be objective observers of interactional processes of our clients. This assumption underlay both our doing diagnostic assessments within a psychiatric orientation and our mapping problem maintenance patterns.

In the '70s this therapist as objective observer/expert position had been supported for family therapists and brief therapists by the framework of systems theory, information processing models, and first-order cybernetics. As brief therapists, we mapped problem maintenance patterns in the language of homeostatic systems and feedback. Shortly thereafter, theoreticians like von Foerster (1982, 1984), von Glasersfeld (1984, 1987), and Watzlawick (1976, 1984) argued against the objective observer position and promoted radical constructivism and second-order cybernetics. Where first-order cybernetics assumed that we could observe homeostatic systems, that is, patterns of problem maintenance, second-order cybernetics argued that we could no longer justify this observing position. The observing therapist always influences the observing, and the observer influence is always part of the observation. In other words, if we as therapists believed in enmeshed families, then that is what we would find. If we used family of origin concepts, then we would find evidence of the cause of the present problem in facts about the family in the past. Constructivists were suggesting that we needed constructs for a self-observing therapy system, constructs for therapists who would be observing the entire system of therapist and client together rather than just the client.

How could we be observers of the client and observers of our own observations at the same time? This self-reflection remained muddled for us until we realized that we needed a nonvisual metaphor in order to make better sense of *self-observing system*. Observational metaphors of scientific objectivity, which always imply a certain spatial-like distance between observer and observed, were no longer useful. Consequently, we adopted communicational metaphors, which imply not unidirectional observation but rather mutual influencing. We decided to drop the metaphor of therapy as research and fixing or healing. We decided to drop the language of observation, objectivity, and information within that metaphor. Instead, we decided to adopt *conversation* as the appropriate new metaphor.* We began to talk about our interactions with clients as conversations rather than interviews.

During this shift, we became uncomfortable with the term *therapy*. Therapy was the label for many discourses based on the notion of an objective observer position, evaluating pathology and deficits. We became convinced

---

*We are grateful to Harlene Anderson and the late Harry Goolishian, who introduced us to thinking of therapy as conversation.

of the need for a new label, a new reference term within the field. While we had been uncomfortable about this term for quite some time and had voiced our concerns in our 1992 book, we had decided in the past that redefining therapy but keeping the word was sufficient. However, with the changes in language and practice that we suggest in the following chapters, we now suggest to helping professionals that the field replace *therapy* with *personal consultation* or some other equivalent term

In the past decade, we have researched the conversation metaphor in poststructural, postpositivist, and postmodern thinking. From our reading, we obtained many inspirations. In the next chapter, we discuss some of those broader inspirations from some postmodern thinking as well as implications of adopting *conversation* and *personal consultation* as guiding metaphors.

CHAPTER TWO

A Dramatic Paradigm Shift within the Field

From Observation to Conversation

Having described our shift from therapy to personal consultation, we here provide a wider context for the additional shifts and changes we will advocate in succeeding chapters. We highlight some of the conceptual shifts and inspirations within philosophy, the social sciences, and the helping professions that distinguish modern and postmodern thinking. These shifts have potential significance for personal consulting.

POSTMODERN IN BRIEF

Postmodern philosophy is often described not as a philosophy on its own but as a critique of modern philosophy or as what is emerging "after" modern philosophy.* Most postmodern writers would resist if not think it impossible to tie a specific meaning to the word "postmodern." Indeed, postmodern writers would not seek to replace modern philosophy systems with another

---

*Postmodern has become an umbrella term that refers to many writers who may otherwise be called poststructural, postpositivist, new pragmatic, feminist, or narrative. Authors often associated with the term postmodern are Bahktin, Baudrillard, Bourdieu, Cixious, Deleuze and Guattari, Derrida, Foucault, Habermas, Irigary, Jameson, Kristeva, Lyotard, Rorty, and Wittgenstein. We realize that in discussing some of the shifts from modern to postmodern we risk oversimplifying and distorting these two terms and some of the ideas within them. Nevertheless, we think it is useful for the reader new to these ideas to have some overall impression of the change from modern to postmodern.

Our interpretation of postmodern inspirations will be biased in that it is selective to the authors we are familiar with, who tend to be from philosophy as opposed to literary criticism.

system. The thrust of postmodern thinking is the recognition that there are many worldviews and that order cannot be imposed by a view from outside or an analysis of what is underneath.

Let us say, however, that what postmodern writers seem to have in common is a reaction to the project of the Enlightenment, the project of establishing a foundation for a universal knowledge that would lead to progress for the human race. They reject the attempt to discover a foundation for universal knowledge, as well as the idea that we can acquire knowledge that is universal and objective. They would instead insist that what we have is practical knowledge, knowledge that is limited to or contingent upon researcher interest, context, and locality. Beyond that, they would also question, if not reject, the idea that the human race has acquired ever greater knowledge and that the race is on an evolutionary track of progress and emancipation from primitive forms.

If modern philosophies (roughly Descartes through Hegel) could be described as having a love affair with the observing subject and the achievements of "man," postmodern philosophies are more tempered by the experiences of world wars, racism, sexism, ecological destruction, and other tragedies resulting from glorified intentions of creating progress. Where modern thinking concerned itself with the question, "What is the foundation of knowledge?" postmodern thinking chooses to abandon the question of universal knowledge and to ask more practical and local questions, for example:

- How do we construct the narratives or beliefs that are relevant to our lives?
- How do other cultural communities construct the narratives or beliefs that are relevant to their lives?
- How do we want our personal and public worlds to be?

These questions represent an attempt to create a practical knowledge rather than a universal theory of knowing. Instead of having a knowledge that is universal and objective, we, as postmodernists, suggest that what we have are narratives and discourses that are shaped by and shape our experience, our history, and our culture. Knowledge is sought not as eternal but as local and pragmatic, in the sense of being the best solution at the present time to a problem that has been generated out of a set of historically mediated understandings and interests (Wachterhauser, 1986).

While postmodern thinking can be seen only as reactive to and skeptical of the quest for a universal foundation for knowledge, we believe that there is an affirmative aspect of postmodern thinking as well. Even though postmodern writers do not propose another philosophical system, they do propose several ways of thinking of what might be useful or lead to new avenues of inquiry. These are not meant to be truth statements, but rather new metaphors to explore. While we draw from many of the ideas of postmodern philosophies, we will highlight only those points that seem most relevant to our work.

POSTMODERN INSPIRATIONS

Postmodern thinking is different and can make a difference in practice. Below we discuss five significant shifts:

1. from universal knowledge to desire and self-assertion
2. from observation of structures and essences to social meaning-making
3. from writer or reader as author to conversation as author
4. from language as representation to languaging constituting values (ethical, pragmatic, aesthetic, and political), relationships, and experience
5. from argument to conversation

From Universal Knowledge to Desire and Self-assertion

Since the time of Descartes in 1637, philosophy and the humanities can be described as seeking an answer to the question, "What is the foundation of knowledge?" Some, empiricists or realists, have answered that the foundation is in the external material world. Others, idealists or constructivists, have said the answer is in the constructs or ideas observers presuppose or bring to the situation.

This has led our disciplines to seek knowledge about the objects of our study. Psychology has sought knowledge about the internal structures and dynamics of the individual psyche or of human behavior. Family therapists have sought knowledge of the structures of families and couples. This paradigm has created the researcher-diagnostician-healer-therapist. Therapists have been trained to make assessments of what is wrong with their clients and to make some treatment interventions.

In the last century, Nietzsche dismissed this Enlightenment project of seeking the foundation for knowledge. He proposed desire rather than knowledge as the principle of his philosophy. At the turn of the century, the pragmatists, James and Dewey, also suggested a shift from seeking a universal knowledge and truth to a practical knowledge that was judged not by truthfulness but rather by the consequences of different ways of thinking. Later, the analytic philosopher Wittgenstein also suggested that we abandon the pursuit of universal foundations.

We use desire and self-assertion as our take-off points. When we use the terms *desire* and *self-assertion*, we are describing them from a postmodern view. We are not referring to self as an essential self, as an entity bounded by body and brain and consisting of cognitions and patterned beliefs and behaviors. Rather we think of self as diverse and taking forms through interaction within contexts. Different "selves" take place in different contexts. We assume that desire and self are social constructions that do not carry meaning necessarily in themselves but vary by context.* Since contexts are rarely the same, the meaning of desire and self-assertion will vary by context. Even within a personal consultation, the meaning of an initially asserted desire will change as the conversation evolves.

How can beginning with desire and self-assertion make a difference?

By beginning with client desire and assuming self-assertion, we are not placing ourselves in an observing or evaluative position with our clients. We are not measuring their experience against normative characteristics of individuals, families or couples. Instead, we are taking the notion of desire and self-assertion not just as philosophical principles but practically as the starting point of our work with clients. Starting with client wants or preferences places us as consultants in a position to join with them in pursuing what they desire or prefer for their lives. As we will discuss in more detail in chapter five, starting with desires and preferences allows us to abandon both problem and solution focuses, as well as the pathology/health distinction.

How can a rethinking of desire and self-assertion make a difference?

Desires and self-assertions are not considered to have bounded meanings. We assume that client-asserted desires, preferences, and wants will change with the context of the conversation. As the context changes—that is, as the consulting conversation changes—the desire can evolve and change as well. An initially stated desire for a spouse to stop drinking can evolve into a desire for trust in the relationship. A mandated client, angry and resentful at being compelled to attend a consultation, may find that what s/he wants and how s/he relates to the consultant changes over the course of the conversation. If the client perceives the consultant as acknowledging what s/he sees as the unfairness of the mandate, the relationship between them changes. The client can become a different "self" who no longer just wants to get even with the boss, but wants to keep her or his job and prove that the boss has an inaccurate assessment.

By thinking of desire or preference in this way, we place the focus on what happens in the interaction between client and consultant. If the client does not agree with the original mandate, the disagreement does not mean that a client is resistant or in denial. The focus remains on what happens between the client and consultant and how the meaning or purpose of the meeting evolves and changes. The client preference in relation to her or his boss may be merely to satisfy the boss in order to keep the job. The client preference in relation to self and family may be to have this requirement out of the way so that s/he can relax on the job, free of the worry of the mandate, and concentrate on doing the job well and providing for her or his family.

*For a full discussion of the postmodern description of self, see Gergen's *Realities and Relationships* (1994).

From Observation of Structures and Essences to Social Meaning-Making

Shifting away from attempts to observe and discover the structures of psyches, families, or relationships, postmodern thought suggests that we all live in a world of linguistic events, that the language we use and choose constitutes our world and beliefs.

If any one of us were the only person on the planet, we might as an individual say to ourselves (if it were possible to have a language to speak to ourselves, given that we would be alone), "I live in a world of objects." This would make sense because a single individual would probably experience herself or himself as surrounded only by objects, if anything at all. However, our current experience is that we live in a social world surrounded by others who are trying to make meaning of their lives and coordinate their actions with each other. The individual self becomes a self-in-language and a self-in-relationship.*

Wittgenstein suggested that we live in a world of linguistic events. We interpret this to mean that we live in a social world of meanings taking place between people within a language that has been generated over time. This is not to say that we are denying objects or the physical world. Living in a linguistic world means that once a human grouping has a patterned way or customed way of using a language, objects can cause or influence the use of the language. In other words, once a professional group decides that "blacking out" is a sign of serious problematic drinking, whether or not someone blacks out determines the group's conclusions about someone's drinking. The world of objects, however, does not determine our language. It does not determine our invention of or use of "problematic drinking" or "black out." The material world does not dictate that blacking out should be used as a criterion.

We take a cue from these later philosophers and their postmodern followers in abandoning universal knowledge or universal truth claims. This means giving up the language of universal human essences or of finding essential characteristics of individuals, families or relationships. For example, in the past we would have assumed that there were universal or essential characteristics to all families. Family was defined in terms of those characteristics. Therapists would evaluate how their client families measured up to this universal definition, which had become a normative definition as well.

A postmodern suggestion is to think in terms of "familinesses" rather than in terms of essences of all families. Rather that describing the family as

---

*We are concerned that in using the word *self*, even in a redefined way as self-in-language or self-in-relation, we will lead readers astray. This redefinition still does not focus enough on the relationship or the space in between selves. Our intention in introducing both of these terms is to focus on the interactional or social space.

having an essence of a two-parent unit with one of more blood-related children, poststructural language would suggest we talk of the many resemblances or variations of familinesses (single parent, adoptive parent, biracial, multiracial, multireligious, etc.) without attempting to define a central, qualifying essence or normative family.

Assuming we live in a world of linguistic events is to say that we live in world of social interpretation of experience. We use the language that is available, that has become used and accepted in a patterned way, and that generates or constitutes our experience. If language is the medium of our experience and at the same time how we communicate and coordinate our actions with one another, then we further assume that language takes place within metaphors and stories. We make meaning of our lives within conversation with others and within ourselves and these meanings carry over time through narratives or stories.

Meaning-making, languaging, knowledging, and creating stories are (a) social, (b) generative, and (c) ongoing. Meaning is organized and stabilized only by punctuating it as such as stories and consensus. We have grouped the words *meaning-making, languaging, knowledging,* and *creating stories* and will treat them as synonymous. We have also presented them all as verbs to highlight that they are fluid and active.* Let us look more closely at what we mean.

Languaging is Social

The talking that we as humans do or the generation of meaning is social. In the past, constructivists assumed that the creation of meaning took place by individuals as they used words and language as perceptual lenses or as frames of interpretation (Maturana, 1978; von Foerster, 1984; von Glasersfeld, 1984; Watzlawick, 1984). However, social constructionists have widened the domain of interpretation, languaging, and meaning-making. Social constructionism is most often associated with the names Jerome Bruner (1986), Nelson Goodman (1978), Kenneth Gergen (1982, 1985, 1994), Rom Harr (1979, 1983), John Shotter (1984, 1993, 1994), Donald Polkinghorne (1988, 1991), Theodore Sarbin (1986), Clifford Geertz (1983), and Charles Taylor (1989). Instead of seeing meaning as an interpretive event by an individual, social constructionism emphasizes how meaning emerges in interaction and in the complex webs of relationships and social processes. Languaging and meaning are social in at least two ways: (1) Languaging takes place within socially created tools (language and signs), which constitute cultures; and (2) it takes place within interaction.

Meaning generation takes place as we talk with someone else or as we talk with ourselves. Even as we read this page, we are in a languaging process with ourselves and the text. We give shape to that experience or we call forth

---

* See Maturana and Varela (1987) for a discussion of using *language* as a verb.

that experience with the tools we have for communicating that experience. Language is the tool we have for thinking of the experience, for making meaning of the experience to ourselves, and for speaking of it to someone else. The experience is shaped within the language. We language with ourselves or with someone else. The speaking is affected not only by the culturally mediated words that we have available but also by the response we perceive from others. In fact, we do not know our own meaning until we put it into words and hear what we have said and hear the other person's response. This dialogue is part of a process of creating meaning.

For example, a young athlete at bat in a baseball game swings at a pitch and hits the ball out of the park for a homerun. During the hitting of the ball he is not talking to himself or anyone else. However, he responds to the events around him given the socially constructed significance. He responds to the pitch as part of the game and hits the ball. Without being familiar with the culturally and socially created meanings, the language of pitch, hit, and ball which in part constitutes the game, the player would not know to hit the ball. After hitting the ball out of the park for a homerun and returning to the dugout, he says to a fellow team player, "That homerun was great. I haven't really hit the ball in over a week." The other player responds and says, "Yeah, but you are turning into a real clutch hitter. If you weren't getting hits at crucial times I don't know if we would be going into the championship." The hitter responds with some enthusiasm, "Yeah, maybe I am."

Both the hitter and the teammate are participating in narrating or meaning-making within the socially constructed rules and meanings of the game of baseball. The words they use, pitch, hit, ball, home run, and clutch hitter, have all been developed as meaningful and capable of communication through the invention, development, use, and consensus over time that these words have a significance that constitutes this context. These words did not always exist and were not always useful. They are social constructions, just as the game of baseball is a social construction. Baseball players, managers, sportscasters, and fans have used these words over time in such a fashion that everyone involved accepts their use and what we all understand by them.

The word *clutch hitter* only takes on use later as the game is developed and more and more people not only use the word but also recognize its use in hearing it. If only the speaker thought it was a meaningful expression, the word would have no use as a communicative tool. The word has to be recognized by more than one person for it to become useful and part of the communicative language surrounding baseball. Along with words, conventions and consensus around voice tones, sentence structures, hand gestures, etc., develop and evolve over time.

Languaging and meaning-making are social not only because the tool we use, language, is a social construction but also because its use takes place as a social action. Meaning generation takes place within interaction or within conversation. The meaning-making above takes place within the conversation between two players. The story emerging between them is of the hitter getting a homerun and being a "clutch hitter" for the team.

Meaning could also be generated in private conversations. As the first player begins to converse with himself, he could be saying, "Man, does it feel great to have a homer again. I was beginning to think I couldn't hit one anymore." The individual is participating and creating a story of himself using language, the socially developed tool available to him. His meaning generation or story creation takes place as he converses with himself.

Here is another example of languaging being social, taken from a personal consultation. A man comes into consultation with concerns about an upcoming custody hearing over his four year-old son. He and his wife have already divorced and they are currently going to a court-ordered mediator over the custody of their only child.

CLIENT: (*with depressed tones*) I am just afraid I will miss some of the best times I could have with my son, those spontaneous times or things that happen on the spur of the moment. My ex-wife says that the best thing for a small boy is to be with his mother and to have a routine with a single home. I want what is best for him but I would like to have as much time as she does.

CONSULTANT: You'd like to have time and the responsibility of his living with you too?

CLIENT: (*somewhat angrily*) Yes, but she says I am selfish and not thinking of the boy. I am only thinking of my needs she says.

CONSULTANT: You would like to think that his spending equal time with you was best for him as well?

CLIENT: Yes, I would like to believe that, but the court people and my ex all say that's nonsense. A young boy should be with his mother!

CONSULTANT: Sounds like you care a great deal about what happens to him. How would it make a difference if you thought equal time was the best thing for your son?

CLIENT: (*with more conviction*) I would not buy into her thinking. I would think there is something equally special about a father's time and that my son would miss something very important to him.

CONSULTANT: How do you mean?

CLIENT: I think I am not as overprotective as she is. I am more encouraging of him, more likely to get him into things with other kids. I think he looks up to me as his father and that would be missing.

In this example, the meaning takes place in the give and take of the client and consultant. Both are participating in narrating his present situation within the socially constructed language around child-rearing and child custody.

Both use the tools of communication that are available to them, the English language and specifically the language of child custody, parenting, and gender roles. While the English language they use is a social construction that has developed and changed over hundreds of years, the specific terms about custody and divorce stand out as more recent additions to the language. The initial client experience is shaped not only by these judicial words but also by some of the cultural expectations that are carried in language about the importance or non-importance of a father's role.

The meaning takes place and changes within the interaction of the consultant and client. While initially the two of them are narrating his desire to have time with his son and his apparent difficulty with his ex-wife's interpretation of that, the meaning continues to evolve within the interaction. The two of them begin languaging as if fathering were special or perhaps as important as mothering.

Languaging is Generative

In our first example, the hitter says to the other player, "That homerun was really great. I haven't really hit the ball in over a week." His use of the word homerun creates the meaning of what happened. If the word were not available, his action of hitting the ball out of the park might be indistinguishable and nonmeaningful to him and the other player. The hitter is beginning to generate a story with his friend of his participating as a baseball player having hit a homerun. They are generating a story of his own emotional reaction and perhaps the reason for his feeling great about the hit.

This narrating or languaging continues as the other player hears his words and responds with, "Yeah, but you are turning into a real clutch hitter. If you weren't getting hits at crucial times, I don't know if we would be going into the championship." He continues the narrating of a story, responding to the hitter's saying he has not hit well in over a week by saying that that the hitter is a clutch player, that is, coming through with a hit in crucial situations. The words *clutch hitter* are distinguishing and calling forth a different significance. The first player may hear an acceptance of his sentence and an expansion or addition to it as the second player adds the topic of "clutch hitter." He may or may not have thought of himself within this term before. If he had thought of himself as a clutch hitter, he may experience this response as affirming. If he had not thought of himself in this way, this may become a new story or new way for him to think of himself.

In the latter example, the father appears very upset about there being only two options for him to make meaning of his situation. He can either give up his time with his son and think that he is doing the best thing for his son or he can think of himself as selfish if he wants equal time with him. Each alternative generates a different experience for him.

As the conversation continues, the conversation generates additional experience. He begins to explore within the conversation how his time with his son might actually be part of his thinking about what is best for his son. The meaning is continuing and is evolving.

With this interchange, a storying or narrating is taking place. The event is being created through the conversation and is generated between the two speaker/listeners. This leads into the notion that meaning-making can be thought of as ongoing.

Meaning-making is Ongoing

While the above examples could be treated as if a finished story or an understanding has been created between the conversants, we are assuming that the meaning or storying could continue. To say that the interchange and what has been created is a finished story is to ignore the fact that there are many more questions that could be asked and much more that could be said.

While we could say that meaning is either ongoing or stable, in the context of personal consultation it is more useful to think of meaning as ongoing and evolving within the conversational space. In the context of a courtroom, it might be more useful to think that some meanings are stabilized within statements and stories. When a jury says that a defendant is guilty, most of us in the courtroom would tend to think of that as a stable meaning and act in accordance with it as a stabilized meaning. The defendant goes to jail, the jury goes home, etc.

In personal consultation we focus on languaging rather than language, on the ongoing evolution of meaning rather than its stabilization, and on storying rather than stories. While we think we have a choice between thinking of meaning as stabilized in a story or as ongoing within continuing conversation, we want to leave out the notion of stories as punctuated or complete as a finished product. So rather than talking about stories and different kinds of stories, problem stories, stories of abuse, solution stories and so on, we want to discuss and use the notion of *storying*. More specifically, we want to talk about co-storying or conversing and how meaning continues to evolve in a conversational space.

How does thinking in terms of social meaning-making make a difference?

By suggesting that we live in a world of linguistic events and a world of meaning-making, we assume that belief, desire, emotion, and action take place within languaging. Language is changeable. Words, sentences, and meanings are indeterminate and change between people and with changes of context.

For example, a client comes in and complains that she is getting into trouble because she is a "driven" person. This self-label has led her to think badly of herself, as if there were something wrong with her. As she explains the situation, she says that her boss has described her as driven and controlling. She adds that this also comes up in committees when she volunteers to chair the meetings. When the committee is given a deadline, she believes it should be honored so she then tries to focus members' attention on the task.

The consultant shares the observation that the client seems rather conscientious and responsible. The client objects that though that may be true and though she is trying to help out her boss and the whole committee, maybe she is not allowing members to talk things out.

The consultant asks, "How are you thinking it might make a difference for people to talk things out?" She explains that maybe not everybody is on the same page just because they are all on the same committee. Maybe they have not all jumped on board with the task and need to decide for themselves.

In this example her concern that she might be driven and controlling has the consequence of making her feel bad and probably of restricting of future actions. The meaning of *driven* and *controlling* changes within the interaction. The consultant shares the observation that the client seems *conscientious* and *responsible*. Perhaps the client feels some acknowledgment of her good intentions, and then she offers a new piece, that maybe she needs to allow members to talk things out.

The context changes as the consultant inquires about the significance of this different action. The context changes from discussing concerns to talking of the significance of a possible action. What emerges from the inquiry is a new meaning, that allowing people to talk things out may be helpful.

This example describes how meaning is socially created, how meaning can change between people, how meaning can change as context changes, and how meaning can generate a different experience. By the end of this short dialogue the client is discussing what she can do in the future that would be more consistent with how she might like to think of herself, that is, conscientious. The tone of the conversation has changed, as has the emotion of the conversation.

This example also brings up the possibility of how she has perhaps initially taken on the gender expectations of her boss. While her boss interprets her behavior as controlling, this may indeed be his own culture-bound expectation of how women should not behave.

From Writer as Author to Conversation as Author

Postmodern thinking shifts the location of meaning or knowledge from the individual observer, as seen through the frames and intentions of that observer, to the domain of the social, that is, to language and conversation.

Conversation is the author.* For social constructionists (Gergen, 1985, 1994; Shotter, 1984, 1993), meaning evolves and takes place in a conversa-

---

*For a more extensive discussion of "conversation as author," see Lynn Hoffman's *Exchanging Voices* (1993).

tional space. The location and punctuation of meaning are widened. Rather than in a single word or statement, meaning is located in the give and take of ongoing interaction, which constitutes the context. As we highlighted in the above examples, the meaning continues to evolve and change. The meaning is not located in either the speaker or listener. Meaning is located and continues to work and evolve in the space between them. It is in this sense that we say the author of the story or conversation is not the individual but rather the conversation.

How does "conversation as author" make a difference?

Conversation as author allows us to think that a new story can emerge between the client and us. Rather than searching for the real meaning within some structural interpretation of what the client is telling us, we assume that between the client and us is the possibility of a new story. This possibility would be beyond what a client might have or what story we, as consultants, might tell of the client's situation. What emerges between us is greater than or different from either of our contributions alone. We do not assume that the professional's interpretation of the client's story is necessarily any better than the client's story. This allows us as consultants not to become too enamoured with our own interpretations or models and not to assume that what the client says means necessarily something about her or him as a person.

From Language as Representation to Languaging Constituting Values (Ethical, Pragmatic, Aesthetic, and Political), Relationships, and Experience.

In the film *Saturday Night Fever*, Tony has a conversation with his dance partner, Angela. While trying to coax him into accepting her as a girlfriend, she tells him that she has decided to have sex with him. Impatient with her attempts to make him a boyfriend, he explains to her that there are two kinds of girls in the world. There are good girls who do not have sex and there are sluts and whores. He says to her that she has to choose which one she is.

Angela looks totally confused. She tells him that all this time he has been trying to get her to have sex with him and now he says that she is being a slut.

A story like this constitutes the prevailing values of sexual relations within the United States in the fifties and into the sexual revolution. For Tony and Angela, their sexual relationship and potential relationship is shaped by this discourse about sex and sexual relationships. Remaining within this discourse constitutes and continues conflicts for both of them and shapes their future relations.

This is a good example of how language, narrative, and metaphor constitute the world we experience. The social world of sexual relations is constituted by the language of sex by unmarried women as equaling slut behavior and no sex as equaling a good woman whom a man would marry. The perpetuation of this metaphor obviously has many consequences for men and women in terms of (1) *ethics*, when, to whom, and whether to have sex, (2) *aesthetics*, what styles are acceptable and considered sexy, attractive, and feminine or masculine, and (3) *politics*, who has the right to define how sexual relationships should be.

In the above dialogue between the consultant and father about custody, the language about custody has potential for constituting not just this man's experience but also that of his son and the boy's mother. For him the language of maternal parenting as being better or right is confining and unfair. The alternative of his getting more of his son's time is valued as selfish by his ex-wife and perhaps is the value of the personnel of the court system. An alternative discourse with paternal parenting being valued as much as maternal appears more to his liking. It allows him to see himself not as selfish but as acting in the interests of his son.

How does languaging as constituting values, relationships, and experience make a difference?

While the above examples bring out some negative consequences, language can also constitute more empowering experiences. If we assume that language, narratives, and metaphors constitute our experience and our clients' experiences, then we can conclude that by clients' participating in a different language, creating a different story, or adopting a different metaphor, they may get what they are seeking or have more of the agency toward what they want. Conversations around a client's acting in the interests of his son or being proactive may create very different experiences for him than conversations around being helpless. Our emphasis is not on the deconstructing or unpacking of problem-oriented stories but rather on the creation of new stories and, therefore, new, desired client experiences. These emerging narratives will be in a language that allows for personal capability and responsibility.

While the idea that language, discourses, and narratives constitute and shape our experience is not new, a postmodern twist on all this is that there is no foundational point from which to evaluate these languages. Just as there is no fixed point in the universe from which to evaluate the speed and direction of the stars and planets, there is no fixed point from which we can objectively evaluate languages, discourses and narratives. We can only discuss one narrative or discourse from the vantage point of another. There is no foundation, meta-point, or God's eye view from which we can objectively evaluate all narratives. We can still make evaluations and analysis of narratives, but only by stating ahead of time what position is being taken in order to make the evaluation. This "situating" of the analysis means describing ahead of time from what position the analysis is being made.

The lack of a foundational point among the varied ways of being and knowing in the world leads to a question, addressed below.

From Argumentation to Conversation

If we do not assume universal or foundational truths or a universal human nature, and if we act as if the world contains many ways of being, desiring and knowing, how can we respect, understand, and coordinate our actions with one another?

One of the solutions offered by Rorty is to adopt the language of conversation and inclusion rather than the language of truth, logic, and exclusion (Hall, 1994, pp. 79-80).

The predominant form of interaction among philosophers over the past four hundred years has been the rhetoric of logical argumentation. This form of rhetoric and interaction makes sense if the members of the interaction share the belief that there is ultimately a true and right answer to philosophical questions. The philosophers would thus argue the truth of their statements and assume that through argumentation the weight of truthfulness would win out. While seeking to find the one answer that was true, the philosophers of the metaphor of Truth worked in exclusionary manners. The belief was that argumentation would lead to the right answer and so the other answers would be discarded.

When philosophers give up the assumption of truth and getting it ultimately right, then the focus and goals of interaction shift from attempting to get it right to something else that needs to be stated. The focus and goals of interaction then become defined and developed by context and situation. If one assumes that there may be many ways of being and desiring, the goal of interaction shifts to seeking to understand, to coordinate with others, and to share what may be useful or valued depending upon the situation.

Rorty's suggestion is that we adopt the metaphor of *conversation*. In other words, if we assume that our goal is not to arrive at the truth but to respect, understand, and coordinate our actions with those who may have different ways of being, desiring and knowing, we need a metaphor that allows for that interchange and is not exclusionary. The metaphor of conversation allows for a different kind of interchange, one where the participants are seen as equals.

The etymology of "conversation" is "to talk with" and has been defined as a friendly interchange of views and sentiments. The metaphor of conversation allows for a respectful, friendly interchange of equals, where the purpose of the interchange can be arranged from within and all points of view can be acknowledged.

How can the metaphor of conversation make a difference?

If we think of personal consultation as an interchange of people who are participating in different ways of being, desiring, and knowing, then conversation seems an appropriate metaphor for that exchange as well. In the following chapters, we will discuss the implications of this shift to post-modern thinking and to the adoption of the metaphor of conversation and the language of personal consultation.

CHAPTER THREE

Inspiring Inquiries
From Assumptions to Explorations

From the concerns about our practice and the inspirations of postmodern thinking we have begun to ask some different questions relevant to our work. These have led to our asking different research questions:

If we suggest that people participate in many and different ways of desiring, knowing, communicating, and storying of their lives, then how can we respect the similarities and differences and still communicate and coordinate our actions?

Assuming that our answer to the previous question is "through conversation," how can we create a space for conversation?

How can we converse with an unknown but evolving purpose? How do we or can we create narratives that are useful and relevant to our lives?

What do our clients and we want?

The first question, *"If we suggest that people participate in many and different ways of desiring, knowing, communicating, and storying their lives, then how can we respect the similarities and differences and still communicate and coordinate our actions?"* arises from a postmodern suggestion that we all live in a world of language, metaphors, and stories. We assume that the languages, metaphors, and stories that people participate in both express and constitute their experience. If we assume there are differences, then how can we attempt to respect and understand? The mode for doing that is *conversation*.

The second question, *"Assuming that our answer to the previous question is 'through conversation,' how can we facilitate a space for conversation?"*

arises from the first question. If we are suggesting that the way that we respect the differences of others and yet still attempt to understand and coordinate with others is through conversation, then we want to research how can we create this space for conversation. If we also suggest that meaning evolves and changes within conversation, then we have another reason for wanting to create a space for conversation. Certainly, clients participate in the creation of conversation and dialogue, but what can *we*, as consultants, do to facilitate our mutually creating this space?

"How can we converse with an unknown but evolving purpose? How do we or can we create the narratives that are useful and relevant to our lives?" While we believe that change takes place within conversation, we believe that we and our clients are engaged in not just any conversation. The conversation with clients is a purposeful conversation. They have a purpose or desire, or it may emerge as we converse. However, the purpose is not predetermined. The purpose(s) evolves between the clients and consultants as the conversation develops and evolves.

From our reading of postmodern philosophy and pragmatism, we decided to abandon the debates over epistemology and the debates over the foundation of knowledge. Taking his cue from Nietzsche and William James, the contemporary author of the new pragmatism, Richard Rorty, suggested: "Instead of saying that the discovery of vocabularies could bring hidden secrets to light, [the pragmatists] said that new ways of speaking could help us get what we want" (1982, p. 150). So, instead of asking, *"How do we know what is real about the client?"* we have decided the more relevant question is, *"What do our clients want and what new ways of speaking or conversing might help?"* If we assume that clients are coming to see us because they want something, and if we assume that how they talk about what they want will change within the conversation, we wonder what desires and possibilities will emerge in the conversation between us.

From our point of view the above four questions are the ones that seem relevant and poignant not just for philosophers but also for our everyday work with clients. From these questions, we created our focal research question:

How can we create a space of dialogue and wonder, where purpose, preferences and possibilities can emerge and evolve? *

Some of the presuppositions within this question are that:

- clients and consultants may participate in different ways or languages of being, of desiring and of knowing,

---

*We are borrowing the word *preferences* from David Epston and Sally Ann Roth (1994) and Jill Freedman and Gene Combs (1996). The term is more appropriate for the open-ended, desire-oriented, and future-oriented nature of our work than the often linearly interpreted term *goal*.

- respecting the differences and strengths of these different ways of being, desiring, and knowing can happen in a space of conversation and with a disposition of wonder,
- the conversation is unique and its purpose(s) is created from within, and
- in this conversational space, client preferences and possibilities can emerge and evolve.

Moving away from the language of observation, assessment, and intervention, we have developed a new language and metaphor for our work. We now consider our approach to be consultative rather than therapizing. Along with that change, our language has shifted from observation, assessment, and intervention to the language of conversation. In other words, we are recreating our work within a notion of conversation that includes the disposition of wonder or curiosity, as well as the activities of invitation, reflection, and encouragement. In making this shift of language, description, and practice, we have borrowed the language of many others. We are indebted to the philosopher Richard Rorty for his notion of conversation and new interpretation of pragmatism (1979, 1982, 1989). We are indebted to the philosopher Ludwig Wittgenstein for his notions of language as social practice, of language games, and of family resemblances (1968). We have appreciated the critique of subjectivity of Foucault (1976, 1980) and Derrida (1978). We have borrowed from the social constructionists Gergen (1982, 1985, 1994) and Shotter (1984, 1993, 1995) ideas on the evolution of meaning within conversation. We have taken inspiration from Harlene Anderson (1997) and Harry Goolishian (Anderson & Goolishian, 1984, 1988), Tom Andersen (1987), Lynn Hoffman (1983, 1985, 1993), and Gianfranco Cecchin (1987), who through their publications fostered our interest in and use of the notions of conversation, dialogue, reflecting, and a not-knowing (curious and wondrous) disposition. We have borrowed the notion of preferences from David Epston and Sally Ann Roth (1994) and Jill Freedman and Gene Combs (1996). Michael White's notion of transparency (1991) allowed us to be open with our clients about our own beliefs and values.

This approach is client-oriented, consumer-oriented, and conversation-oriented. The assumptions that we now make about our practice are not intended to be truth statements. We are subscribing to the ideas not because former ways of thinking are no longer true or helpful, but to see how they will create more desirable forms of practice and open up new avenues for us and for our clients. Postmodern thinking appears to have better fit with the situations and problems of practice at the present time. Given the diversity of people with whom we work and their different ways of being and making sense of their world, we look for ways of working that respect the uniqueness of people and their differences and allow us to be helpful in a way that is unique to each.

Below is a list of inquiries that suggest both postmodern ideas and possibilities of inquiry.* Each question is simultaneously a working suggestion and an inquiry. In the past we created a list of assumptions that guided our work. We found that such a list made possible clarity and coherence in our thinking; however, we also found that sometimes such a list of assumptions closed off inquiry in the sense that the list assumed already determined practices and answers to problems. This new list is intended to remind you that these are not truth statements. They are, after all, not statements at all. They are possibilities of inquiry with no predetermined answer. As we explore the possibilities and consequences of the varied answers to each inquiry, we are reminded that our approach is "in-becoming," and not a finished model or fact. We hope that this list encourages you, too, to engage in a continuing process of inquiry and creativity rather than approaching personal consultation as a finished model to be mastered.

INSPIRING INQUIRIES

Inquiries about meaning-making and conversation

- How can we act as if meaning-making is a conversational event?
- How can we create a space of conversation, a space of dialogue and wonder, so that preferences and possibilities can evolve?

Consultant-client disposition

- How can we facilitate a disposition of wonder, curiosity, and openness both for ourselves and our clients?

Desire as conversational process

- How can we "preference"? How can we facilitate creative conversations with an evolving sense of purpose?

Storying

- How can we focus on storying rather than stories?

Purpose of personal consultation

- How can we act as if the overall purpose of consultation is client agency, preferences, and possibilities about what the client wants, and not necessarily client action?

---

*The inspiration for presenting a list of inquires rather than assumptions comes from Jill Freedman and Gene Combs, who in *Narrative Therapy* (1996) used a list of questions as the format for presenting guidelines for practice.

Purpose of questions
- How can we act as if questions are tools of listening and for inviting conversations of difference?

Consultation membership
- How can we act as if our clients include any and all who want something?

Diversity
- How can we acknowledge and invite other relevant voices into the conversation?

INSPIRING INQUIRIES

Inquiries about Meaning-Making and Conversation

How can we act as if meaning-making is a conversational event?

With the suggestion that meaning-making is a conversational event, we express our curiosity about how it would be different or helpful to think of change as taking place within conversation, within the space of give and take between consultant and client. We assume that meaning-making takes place within conversation, where words and meanings are always in the process of becoming.

This means that the meaning of a statement is fixed neither in the intention of the speaker nor in the correspondence, or lack thereof, of the statement to an external Truth. While the statement may be an expression of the speaker, its meaning is not fixed in the intention or experience of the speaker. Rather, it continues to evolve as the statement is heard, responded to, and then responded to by the speaker. Punctuation is expanded, and meaning constantly deferred. As listeners, we approximate understanding and seek to understand while realizing that understanding in a complete sense is never possible. This is an open-ended exploration.

Here is an example of how meaning evolves within conversation: A client reports that one thing she wants from the consultation is ". . . to feel less depressed and apathetic." This statement that what she wants from consultation is to feel less depressed and apathetic invites an infinite number of responses and/or inquiries. Each response can reflect something very different and invite even further inquiry rather than a searching for facts.

A response from us of, "So you are feeling a lack of energy?" might be responded to with, "No, it is not a lack of energy. I just feel discouraged about my husband."

The consultant's response then might be, "So, you would like something to be different in your relationship with your husband?"

The conversation between this client and consultant could continue with another response, such as, "Yes, I would like him to be more responsive, I would like to feel that our relationship is growing."

Each statement or question takes on meaning and new understanding yet defers closure and invites further inquiry or meaning-making. The meaning or story emerging here is emerging between them and is not the product of either of them alone. It is the product of each statement, response, and response upon response. It is neither the client's story nor the consultant's story. Meaning is produced by the conversation, and the conversation itself might be thought of as the author in the sense that the storying is bigger than and different from either person's contribution alone (Hoffman, 1993). A conversation between this client and another person or a different consultant could lead to a different conversation and different meanings might emerge.

Conversation-as-author is different from thinking of consultation as information-gathering about some qualitative state of the client. In everyday talking, we generally assume that language represents the facts of either our experience or of the world around us. In the above conversation, we assume that the conversants above are talking as if their words are codes for inner states or facts in the outside world. We further assume the meaning is never finished and that it will evolve in the give and take of the conversation.

By assuming that meanings occur and evolve within conversation, we focus our work and further inquiry primarily on the conversational domain and what happens between client and consultant, rather than on what is taking place within the client or in the factors external to the client. This means that, instead of focusing on gathering factual information about the client in order to assess if the client really is depressed or apathetic, we are asking questions in order for story creation to take place. If we assume further that some stories may be more helpful or useful to the client, it behooves us to join the client in the creation of such stories.

How can we create a space of conversation, a space of dialogue and wonder, so that preferences and possibilities can evolve?

We assume that meaning evolves in an atmosphere in which the norm is openness, wonder, and inquiry. Such an atmosphere occurs easily when conversants allow themselves to be open to newness and difference. This atmosphere is enhanced by assuming that all members of a consulting meeting are not holding fast to any predetermined notions, but are instead assuming a non-normative position of curiosity and not-knowing (Anderson & Goolishian, 1988; Cecchin, 1987).

If we enter a relationship assuming ahead of time that we know what is right or best for our clients, then we are already closing off possibilities, as well as our ability to be open and understanding. As soon as we assume we understand, then curiosity ceases. We do not assume that one way of being or desiring is necessarily any better than any other. We approach the consulting relationship holding whatever ideas we have with a tentative hand and allow ourselves to be open to new or different ideas.

Consultant-Client Disposition

How can we facilitate a disposition of wonder, curiosity, and openness both for ourselves and our clients?

We assume again that newness and possibilities have more of a chance of emerging when we attempt to be open and nondogmatic. So we approach each consulting situation as if it were a totally new situation. We avoid making a list of questions and even eschew the idea that we have some privileged access to what is good for the client. Ours is not the curiosity of a detective, but an ever open curiosity about what the client is saying and what s/he is not saying, or maybe has not said yet. We try to be as curious and open as a five-year old, as if everything is and can be new.

Here is as example of this position:

CLIENT: The reason I am here is because I've learned that I'm a codependent.

CONSULTANT: How do you mean?

CLIENT: My previous therapist before I moved told me that I'm codependent and too focused on helping my husband. She said that I should be focused on myself and leave him.

CONSULTANT: Really? You think so too?

CLIENT: Well, I do love him and I can't seem to stop worrying about him.

CONSULTANT: Tell me more.

CLIENT: I know he drinks too much and I know I should leave him but he's a good man most of the time.

CONSULTANT: Sounds like you wish the best for him.

CLIENT: I do. I do wish he could stop.

CONSULTANT: How are you hoping that would make a difference?

CLIENT: Hmm. I wouldn't worry about his safety and maybe we could have a family life.

CONSULTANT: That's what you are wanting—his safety and a family life.

This short dialogue suggests that a disposition of curiosity and respect can be facilitated by abandoning agendas of diagnosis, intervention, or client's need to change. Any such agendas hinder the consultant's ability to listen. Instead, the consultant seeks to respect the client's intentions and efforts. The consultant seeks to understand what the client wants and what the client may want the consultant to understand. This generally leads to a sense of mutual inquiry rather than a pursuing of some interview protocol or strategy.

Desire as Conversational Process

How can we "preference"? How can we facilitate creative conversations, with an evolving sense of purpose?

While everyday conversations and consulting conversations may share similarities of being open and spontaneous events, we assume that consulting relationships need to have relevance specific to the client and ourselves. We therefore assume that consulting conversations have an evolving sense of purpose but not a predetermined purpose. The purpose(s) of the conversation emerges between the consultant and client, not from a normative protocol such as *DSM-IV* (American Psychiatric Association, 1994) or from a prescriptive treatment plan.

We use the notion *an evolving sense of purpose*, because we do not know what the purpose is ahead of time and because we assume that even the client's initial statements of what s/he wants will evolve and change. Furthermore, we assume that purpose and relevance are part of the meaning-making that occurs. In other words, the purpose or relevance of the conversation is likely to change and evolve as the conversation continues.

Using the words *preference, purpose,* and *relevance* as nouns implies that these words refer to endpoints or stabilized events with a concreteness that may be more constraining than helpful. This is why we use the word *preference* as a verb and talk about the consultant and client as *preferencing*. In the past we used the construct *goal* to give purpose and direction to our meetings with the client. We found, however, that the word *goal* felt confining, because a goal is most often thought of as a stabilized meaning or concrete product of focused actions. As we tried to redefine this word as a process, i.e., *goaling*, we found that the notion of goal is too steeped in linear ways of thinking, even when redefined as a process.

A metaphor for thinking of goals as concrete events within linear thinking is golf. The goal of each hole of golf is sinking the ball in the hole. All efforts then are centered around this ball being in the hole, and the purpose is not resolved until that happens. Thinking forward in this fashion can be useful. Having an idea of what one wants to happen is more useful than having no idea or focusing only on what one does not want. This notion of goal as endpoint is useful, particularly with concrete physical events. However, the metaphor tends to lead to instrumental or linear thinking; that is, one tries to identify linear, behavioral steps to accomplish the goal. Linear thinking often breaks down in the process of figuring out what would be the next step and how to make it happen. What gets left out in the goal as endpoint thinking is the nonlinear complexities or spontaneity of human events.

When a couple comes in and says that they want more "trust" in their relationship, they may have no idea what they mean by "trust." To attempt to specify trust in concrete terms might be nearly impossible. They may only be able to guess and recognize what they want as it begins to happen. It may not be something they can identify ahead of time and then devise some plan for accomplishing it.

Another limitation of thinking of goals as targets can be that, in attempting to specify the goal, the consultant can become so intent on satisfying criteria for a well-specified goal that s/he does not listen to the client.

We have found it useful to adopt the word *preference* instead of goal and to think of purpose, relevance, and preference as spontaneous conversational processes rather than targeted objects or events. When we use preference as a verb, the word becomes consistent with our notion of conversing. In other words, preference ceases to be a concrete event in a single moment of time and instead is thought of as conversational process. Preference becomes "preferencing." Preferencing becomes conversing between people with the assumption that relevance and purpose will arise within the conversation and between them rather than being an object possessed by the client before s/he came to the meeting. Preferencing becomes an activity between client and consultant that is not imposed from outside by cultural beliefs or by normative protocols within our own field. Preferencing becomes authored by the conversation, rather than by any individual, normative protocol, technique, or decision tree.

The assumption that purpose evolves within the conversation also brings up the issue of consultant intentionality. While we have stated that conversation is created by the consultant being open and not predetermining how the conversation should go, we do assume that every consultant or therapist approaches a meeting with some intention. Our overall intention upon creating a conversation is to facilitate an open space where clients can converse creatively about their concerns, desires, and preferences. We assume that clients come to see us because they want something or they want something to be different. Again, this is an approach based on an assumption of client desire. We assume, therefore, that if a client states that s/he wants something from coming to see us or wants to engage in some purposeful discussion, then we have the beginning of a creative conversation.

Inquiring and Storying

How can we focus on storying rather than stories?

The narrative metaphor is prevalent in postmodern thinking.* In contrast to theories of realism, facts, and entities, the narrative metaphor promotes the idea that experience is constituted in language and maintained within stories or narratives. The thrust here is that we all live within socially

---

* It would be nearly impossible to list all of the authors who have used the term *narrative* in its various uses. Key figures for us have been Barthes, 1974, E. Bruner, 1986, J. Bruner, 1986, 1990, 1991, Geertz, 1983, Gergen, 1994, Lyotard, 1979, 1984, White and Epston, 1990.

created and socially shared narratives. These stories are not factual in the objective or real sense, but they provide meaning and coherence to our lives.

As with preferencing, we like to use story as a verb. Rather than focus on client stories, as if they were enclosed entities, we focus on the storying or creative inquiring that takes place between client and consultant, and between clients. This means we do not focus on solution stories, or problem stories, or resource stories. While not denying the differences created by talking of stories versus facts or systems, we emphasize the possibilities of process, that is, creative conversing or storying. We highlight mutual narrating or creating of stories. Again, this is consistent with our focus on conversing, preferencing and meaning-making.*

From a structural view, we would assume that a story is complete and that a problem story needs to be changed or deconstructed. From a narrative view, we focus on storying rather than stories and the story does not become an object to be changed. Stories are always changing in the telling, the hearing, the inquiring of, and different telling.

One reason for preferring storying over story is that the word *story* can become a bounded entity that needs to be changed. For example, a client says that she is concerned that she is codependent. She talks about how she often gets together with her mother, and they go out for dinner. She states that while at dinner her mother gets drunk and she herself participates in this by paying for the drinks, listening to her mother's intoxicated stories, and getting pretty high herself. Upon hearing that story, many clinicians would assume that it represents a personality structure of dependence and an interpersonal structure of codependence. These listeners would assume that the client's story represents underlying individual and interpersonal structures in need of change.

Others would not say that the story represents a structure. They would assume that the story is a problem story that has emotional, political, and pragmatic consequences. They would assume that the story needs to be changed. Those of a normative persuasion might assume that a therapist should help edit this story according to norms of what is a proper use of alcohol and what is a normal relationship with one's adult parent. Others, not of a normative persuasion, might hear this story as the client's experience. They might assume that this is a problem-laden story that needs to be changed. While they would not have normative criteria of how the story should be different, they would work as if the story were complete and in need of transformation.

By focusing on *storying* rather than stories, we would assume that a client's telling us of a situation is an incomplete story. If we were to focus on *the story* we would be assuming that the meaning was complete within the

---

* Throughout the text we use the words *inquiring, narrating, storying, conversing, creating,* and *meaning-making* interchangeably.

story. By focusing on *storying* we assume that the client is beginning to tell us something that is of concern to her. What she has told us so far leaves a great deal of room for further questions and for the storying to go in many directions. The story-telling opens up more questions and more than one story to be told/created. Focusing on storying or inquiring allows us to assume that a story of more personal agency can be created.

We assume that, by the way we listen and attend to different things, the same story that she told before is not going to be told. In our presence the storying or telling of stories is already a different telling from what the client might have said before or with someone else. The difference in telling may be the experience of saying what she wants without judgment by the listener. A different story might emerge, one that the client was not aware of before. With conversation, rather than the client, as the author there are many possible stories. So rather than focusing on *the* story, we concentrate on inquiring.

From a position of inquiry we might ask ourselves and the "codependent" woman, "What makes you want these situations to be different?" "Is this different for you to realize that you do not like these dinners to go this way and you to want something different for yourself or your mother?" "What makes you value this relationship enough to want to have a different time with your mother?" "Are there times now when dinners or times together go more to your liking?" Any of these inquiries and their responses might open up a different telling, a different listening, and a different experience.

What we frequently do, as we will discuss later, is merely accept clients' telling of a situation of concern. As they complete the telling to their satisfaction, we may not inquire about the concern at all. We might just express our support for their disappointment with how badly things are going and then ask how they would like things to be. This inquiry into what s/he wants steps around the whole problem story/solution story distinction. We accept her expression of concern and then move into what the client wants. There is no need then to subvert or deconstruct the problem story.

Purpose of Personal Consultation

How can we act as if the overall purpose of consultation is client agency, preferences, and possibilities about what the client wants, not necessarily client action?

This question reverts to the inquiry about "preferencing." We assume that whatever brings a client to consultation has been constructed within language, within some conversation with others or themselves. We also believe that this reason or purpose continues to evolve within conversation.

Problem-solving approaches generally make some instrumental assumptions. In other words, these approaches assume that clients need to take some action in order to solve a problem. Or, they may assume that clients need some insight about the problem in order to take some action. The opposite assumptions would be that client actions are not relevant or helpful and that somehow client goals can be reached without their taking action of some sort. What we suggest, however, is that it is not a given that clients need to take action or that client action should be the goal of the consultation.

We suggest that the meaning of a situation evolves and changes within conversation. We hope that the conversation evolves so that clients who before may have believed that they were helpless now would feel that they have options or possibilities. Some of those possibilities may include different actions, or the possibilities might make action unnecessary. While we assume that all meaning can have pragmatic and political consequences, we do not assume that client action necessarily has to be one of the consequences and we do not assume the responsibility of getting the client to take some action.

Previously, while working from a strategic orientation, we thought that change and learning took place through doing. We have not necessarily given up that way of thinking. We still think that people change through doing and that learning can be accomplished through doing. However, in our strategic orientation we often assumed that our clients were stuck. We thought and made assessments from the assumption that clients were coming to see us because they were in a problem state, concluding that they had to do something to move out of that problem state. It became our goal to move them to take that action.

We now assume that, while clients may come to see us with problem stories, these stories are fluid and changing in the course of their conversing with us. Our focus is on the inquiring. So, rather than thinking that the story is stable or that the clients are stuck, we assume that meaning or stories are changing as clients converse with us. If we assume that the clients' concerns, hopes, and desires in coming to see us are constructed within language, then those concerns, hopes, and desires are seen as changing while they converse with us. Through this conversation with us, the meaning evolves and changes in such a way that the clients leave with some more sense of agency or possibilities. This may lead to their taking some action or different action, but that is not our sole focus within the consulting meeting. The hope is that preferences will evolve in such a way that clients recognize choices and actions they can take if they decide to.

Purpose of Questions

How can we act as if questions are tools of listening and for inviting conversations of difference?

We used to assume that the purpose of asking questions was to gather information about clients. We imagined ourselves to be clinical versions of Sergeant Joe Friday from the old "Dragnet" series—we wanted just "the facts." We assumed that when we had obtained the appropriate facts about the problem or goal, we could put that information together in a meaningful fashion, an assessment, which would then determine our course of action for treatment.

We also used to ask questions in a rhetorical sense, with an answer already in mind. When we asked a couple, "Do you think that your son is engaging in drugs because he can't stand the tension from your fighting?" we generally had an answer already in mind.

Now that our conversations with clients are not interviews for information, we ask questions with different reasons. They are *not* asked to :

- gather information,
- make an assessment,
- validate a hypothesis,
- get the client to do something or to do something different,
- solve a problem,
- gain insight,
- motivate action, or
- be helpful.

From a position of curiosity and wonder *with* the client and *from within* the conversation, questions are asked in attempts to understand what the client is saying and to inquire with the client about what the client wants and relevant possibilities. This does not prohibit us from having a list of useful questions. They are *possibilities within conversation.* Chapters in the remainder of this book are devoted to useful distinctions within conversation. These distinctions can be used within questions. For example, some of the questions that we find useful are:

- What do you want from coming here?
- How would that make a difference to you?
- What might be some signs to you that that was happening?

If we thought of ourselves as interviewing for information, we would ask these questions in sequence and take the client's answers as information. If we thought of these questions as part of a methodology, we would ask them in order. However, to us these questions are useful depending on the conversation and as ways to explore the conversation. Their use is not predetermined as necessary for a meeting to be complete or successful and they do not determine the conversation: the conversation determines when and if these questions might be useful and appropriate. While the questions do not determine the conversation, we will talk about them and stress their usefulness throughout this book.

We realize that there is a danger, even if you think of these questions as tools for conversation, that the tools will heavily influence the directions of curiosity. As Milton Erickson used to say, if the only tool you have is a hammer, then most of your clients will look like nails. Nonetheless, we want to highlight the potential usefulness of these questions and the ways of thinking the questions represent when used within a conversation. We would like to stress that questions are only recognized as useful in hindsight. In other words, if asking a question facilitated an open conversation, then it was useful. However, we cannot know that ahead of time. Usefulness can only be determined in hindsight.

Imagine a consulting conversation to be like an improvisational jazz session. The members of the session act spontaneously with one another. The jamming is spontaneous and what the musicians do arises from the jam. At the same time, different musicians have riffs and different sounds that they are familiar with, and they bring them to this spontaneous event. So, too, in conversations with our clients, we approach the conversation as a spontaneous event, but we have questions that we bring to the conversation. We use them as the conversation invites them and they become possibilities within conversation.*

In a pragmatic sense, let us stress also that questions are used to express consultant curiosity, to let clients know that we are interested and taking what they say seriously, and to invite conversations of difference. Questions are ways of listening to the extent that they are responses to what the client said and reflect curiosity about what more could be said. Social constructionists Shotter and Gergen speak to this topic with different words. Shotter (1995) speaks of this as *responsive listening*. Thus, the meaning of a client's statement is put in a conversational context by the listener's response, in this case a question. Gergen (1994) calls this conversational process *supplementation*. As ways of listening, questions are seen as responses to what the client has said. From the client's experience, the questions can be experienced as signs of the consultant listening, as attempting to understand and take seriously what they as clients have already said, and as acknowledging what the clients have already said as important and relevant to their meeting.

For example, a client may say, "Lately, it's an effort just to walk my dog." A consultant may ask in response, "Mmmm, sounds pretty tough. . . . How do you manage to do that?" The client may be expressing here his sadness and discouragement that things are going so badly that even a simple task like walking his dog seems like a major effort. The question by the consultant flows from this hearing of what has been said. The question may be heard by the client as acknowledging the extreme difficulty of the situation, as taking the difficulty seriously, and as an expression of curiosity about that effort in those difficult circumstances.

While questions are seen as ways of listening, they are also seen as tools of curiosity and creation of difference. In the above example, the question,

---

*We would like to thank Michael Banks for this improvisational jazz metaphor.

"How did you manage to do that?" acknowledges the difficulty of the situation. It also reflects curiosity about what may not have been said yet, or what could be storied more, that is, how he managed to mount the effort despite the difficulty. We call this asking of questions *curiosity of difference* or *inviting conversations of difference*.

The client's experience of this question could be acknowledgment of the difficulty, a sign of the consultant listening, and a sign of the consultant's further curiosity about what more could be said about a different aspect of the emerging story. The conversation may then go in the direction of how the client acted competently, even in these difficult circumstances.

Consultation Membership

How can we act as if our clients include any and all who want something?

A personal consulting group is defined by those declaring that they share purposes or desires. The membership and purpose are declared from within. The group's organization is created by declaring a purpose or concern, even if the group does not agree about the definition of the concern, what they want, or the means to getting what they want. This includes the consultant by the consultant's agreeing to work with the client(s) on what they want.

An example is a man who came to see us because of his concern about a recent incident in which he struck his two young daughters with a plastic baseball bat. He stated he was very frightened and concerned about his losing control and he wanted to figure out what he could do to make this never happen again. He also related that his wife had called the police during this incident and that Child Protective Services had become involved. While he knew his wife was angry with him and his daughters were frightened, he was sure that they wanted him to return home.

The consulting group consisted of those who stated that they wanted a change. This included the father, his wife, the probation officer who became involved after the man's court appearance and us as consultants. The father attended the sessions while the wife attended some sessions and the probation officer was involved by phone.

All of them became involved and participated. Each of them stated that they wanted something to be different. Each of them became involved by their initiation rather than our asking or insisting. The group became defined by their concern about what had happened and each person's desire to change the situation. The group was defined by their languaging about what they wanted.

When clients ask, "Who should attend?" we answer, "Everyone who is concerned about the situation."

This is different from therapy models that determine the membership and purpose of the therapy by some authority or criteria established outside the therapy session. Traditional organizational therapy models assume that the problem results from some deficiency in a socially defined unit such as an individual psyche, a family, or couple. These models then assume that therapist's role is to treat the disorder or dysfunction within these structures. These models then assume that the membership of the therapy system should be the therapist and whatever unit the therapist determines is the source of the problem. For us, the reverse is true. The languaging about a goal determines who will participate and who becomes the personal consulting group.

This defining from within is similar to Anderson and Goolishian's problem-determined system (1984). They stated that the therapy system is determined within language by those who state that there is a problem. The treatment system is a problem-organizing and problem-dissolving system. While we share the notion that the personal consulting group is determined and defined from within, we prefer to speak of the group as a preference-determined system. The personal consultant and client form this group as they language around the purpose for their meeting. The membership of the group is not constant. Some people may lose their interest, or their interest may be satisfied after a meeting or two. In other situations, another's interest in attending may come to the fore.

For example, when one couple came to a first meeting, the husband said that he was concerned about his wife's dissatisfaction with him. He was willing to do almost anything possible to change her attitude and keep his marriage together. She stated that she was concerned about his talking about killing himself whenever she talked about divorce. She was not interested in keeping the marriage together, but rather in his becoming nonsuicidal so that she could leave. In that first meeting, she decided that he would have to take the responsibility for continuing his life and that she could not be ruled by the threat or possibility of suicide. She decided not to return for another meeting. He, on the other hand, was still determined to win her back. He decided to continue coming to the consultation to pursue winning her back. In this situation, the membership changed as the purposes evolved and changed.

Another example was a woman who came in and said that she was feeling depressed. As the conversation continued, she said that she was concerned about the lack of communication and connection within her marriage. By the end of the meeting, she asked if it would be okay if her husband joined her next time. I* asked if she thought he was concerned about matters between them as well. When she said yes, I concurred with her that she might want to ask him. He came the next time and expressed his desire for his marriage to be better. The membership expanded as he joined with her and the consultant around a shared preference.

*When we use the singular pronoun, readers can assume that either of us was the personal consultant.

We make the assumption that people coming to us for personal consultation are coming for some reason or purpose, even if they cannot state that purpose clearly. We also assume that the purpose in their coming to see us may and probably will change over time. The purpose usually evolves and changes as they converse about what they want. This evolving purpose and preferencing marks how these conversations are different from casual conversations. The conversation is purposeful and pragmatic. The purpose is determined from within by those who join the conversation.

This conversation may be about what the clients want or how they want their experience to be and/or how they will know they are either experiencing it or making progress toward it. We believe that focusing on these areas facilitates the generation of new meaning and experience.

Diversity

How can we acknowledge and invite other relevant voices into the conversation?

Within a structural or organizational framework, the problem is assumed to be a deficiency within a structural unit like an individual, a couple, or a family. The therapist determines which social unit is the source of the problem and should be treated. The effect of this has been that relevant voices have been pushed to the side. The expert therapist is the predominant, if not the dominant, voice. Opinions and voices outside of the therapist-determined unit of treatment are discounted. A client's complaints about a spouse would be reinterpreted to be somehow statements about the client rather than taken on face value. What this means for us is that oftentimes opening the space within the conversation for voices or points of view that have not been heard can introduce difference and possibilities for the client. We then have conversations with multiple authors.

An example is a young man who came in concerned about his anxiety with his family. He stated that he was gay and had been out for several years with his friends but not with his family. Despite his having a loving partner, he had never acknowledged this man as his partner to his mother or extended family. At family functions, he was nervous and anxious when relatives asked about his personal life. When I asked how he would like them to react to him, he said that he would like them to be okay with his being gay. We discussed whether he would like them to merely tolerate his sexual preference or if he would like them to celebrate and be excited for him. He stated that ideally he would like them to happy and excited for him but that he would accept their being tolerant. We discussed for a while how he would know that his relatives would be tolerant. He replied that if they did not make any negative comments and if they were okay with his bringing his partner to family functions. I asked why he wanted to do this, and he stated that he loved his family and that he did not want this to come between him and them. I then invited the reflections of his family through him. I asked, "If your mom and aunt were listening in on this conversation, what do you think they would say?" He was somewhat surprised when he said that he thought they would say they were happy for him that he had found some-one.

Inviting other voices into the conversation can often contribute to mean-ingful difference for the client or open conversations beyond the scope of the meeting.

With the above inspiring inquires, let us now look to some of their pragmatic consequences and return to our research question: "How can we create a space of dialogue and wonder, where purpose, preferences, and possibilities can emerge and evolve?"

CHAPTER FOUR

Creating a Space
of Dialogue and Wonder

From Interview to Conversation

With regard to our research question, "How can we create a space of dialogue and wonder, where purpose, preferences, and possibilities can emerge and evolve?" we offer several metaphors. Our overarching metaphor for personal consultation is *conversation*. We use *conversation* to describe the context, our role and actions, and what happens between consultant and client. With regard to the second part of the research question, "where purpose, preferences, and possibilities can emerge and evolve?" we offer the additional metaphors of *visualization, mind-mapping,* and *story-writing* of preferences, possibilities, and optimism. These additional metaphors will be discussed in later chapters.

Within the conversation metaphor, we speak of three dispositions, namely, (1) being "curious with," (2) being reflective, and (3) being encouraging. These dispositions are sensitivities and activities that we as consultants bring to the conversation. Our hope is that these dispositions help to foster a conversational space and that they will be a mutual part of the conversation. In other words, by our approaching the meeting with these dispositions, we hope to create a conversation whereby the interaction between the consultant and client is characterized as mutually inquiring (curious), reflective, and encouraging. Each of these dispositions will be discussed in turn. Being curious will be discussed in this chapter through chapter nine. Reflecting and encouraging will be discussed in chapter ten.

CONVERSATION

Conversation provides inspiration for new ways of thinking and interacting with clients. In conversation, two or more people talk *with* each other. All members of the conversation are free to be there, free to share whatever they choose to share, free to ask what they want, and free to contribute in the way they choose. The direction, the restrictions, the meaning, and purpose arise out of the conversation.

This is in contrast to an interview by a newspaper reporter, where the reporter has an agenda for a story that s/he wants to get. The reporter asks all the questions and the meaning or interpretation is finally in her/his hands. This is also in contrast to a therapy assessment, where the assessor sets the agenda and asks all the questions. The questions asked are either predetermined by some interview protocol, such as the *DSM-IV* (American Psychiatric Association, 1994), or by the goal of the interviewer to gather information to be evaluated against some normative standard. This is also in contrast to a researcher, who already has in mind hypotheses, distinctions, constructs, and questions with which the researcher will not only conduct the interview but also interpret the data. In all of these interview situations, there is an implicit understanding of expertise inherent in the position of writer of the newspaper story, evaluator of the dysfunctional mental or family health, or interpreter of the data. With this implicit or explicit understanding comes acceptance of hierarchy and roles.

Within the metaphor of conversation, we assume a norm of equality and mutuality. The personal consultant is not assuming the position of expert or of assessor of what is good or healthy functioning. The personal consultant adopts the position of conversant. We act as an equal participant and thereby contribute to an atmosphere of dialogue.

In workshops, we have suggested an exercise for participants to experience some of these differences between interviews and conversations. In the initial part of the exercise, we ask participants to pair up, with one person pretending to be an intake worker and the other pretending to be a client. We set the context as one where the intake worker is required to find out and make some assessment of how serious a drinking problem the client has. The intake worker is told to ask whatever questions s/he has to ask or to do what is necessary to find out and make this determination. The intake worker feels some pressure to get this information.

We give the person role playing the client free rein to play whomever s/he wants. The participant can be her or himself, with an imagined drinking problem or not.

We ask that in either role, the intake worker or the client, the persons monitor what the experience is like. They are to be aware of what adjectives they would use to describe their experience within those roles.

Often the participants describe several experiences. The intake workers describe feeling intrusive and uncomfortable with having to ask interrogating style questions, almost like a prosecuting attorney with a reluctant witness. They describe how strange it is to be asking questions to satisfy some agenda.

They also describe that they feel frustrated. Often the client seems evasive and vague in response to questions about drinking. Facing evasiveness and vagueness, participants respond with various tactics. Some attempt to be confrontive. They describe trying to be up front by saying that there must be a problem in their drinking. Otherwise, why are they there? This attempt usually is met with increased evasiveness.

Other participants attempt to be more strategic. They try a little empathy first, before asking a leading question. They may say something like, "It sounds like you are really under a lot of pressure. With all that pressure, do you occasionally have a drink to find relief and relax yourself?" Sometimes both intake worker and client describe how this strategy works in getting the client to begin talking about drinking.

Those in the client role often describe feeling defensive with questions about drinking, especially when their perception is that drinking is not a problem. The clients describe feeling intruded upon and judged by this worker, who seems to be assuming, given the questions, that they must have some problem with drinking. They describe feeling intruded upon, judged, not listened to, and interrogated.

As we ask members in both roles for more descriptions of what happened, they describe a hierarchy of roles. In one role, the intake worker assumes the privilege of asking all the questions, of being able to make some evaluation or judgment; the client's role is to cooperate.

We then ask workshop participants to participate in a second exercise, saying that afterward we will contrast the two experiences. We ask that they pair up with the same person but this time they are to pretend that they do not know each other. They are to pretend that they are meeting each other for the first time at a party given by a mutual friend. They are both going to this party with no agenda. Neither is going there to meet the person of her or his dreams or to pick someone up. They are going to this party just to have fun. They meet each other when they are both up at the buffet table about to sample some of the food. They strike up a conversation. The participants again are asked to monitor this experience and to prepare to describe what it was like at the end of the exercise.

Participants describe that this time they had fun. They might report some discomfort with the lack of structure or roles; however, very soon they both began to find things in common and attempted to get to know each other. They describe how initially they might have talked about the food or the host of the party but quickly began to talk about or ask about each other. What they talked about seemed to flow from between them, what they were both interested in, or from the conversation itself.

They also describe the freedom in the second exercise, that there was freedom to ask or to share what they wanted and to leave or stay. This led them to say that the relationship seemed more mutual. There was no expectation from outside the conversation about what was to happen or what should happen. The questions they asked arose from within the conversation and from their curiosity arising at the moment. They were not predetermined by some interview format or strategy.

Ironically, they describe how they got to know the other person better in the second exercise than in the first.

While these exercises are staged to bring out the advantages of the second exercise, the contrast brings out many of the advantages we see in adopting conversation as a metaphor for personal consultation.

Within conversation, there is mutuality of roles rather than a hierarchy where one member is assumed to have a position privileged by assumed expert knowledge. As in personal consultation, the conversant is not assumed necessarily to have expert knowledge about human life. She or he may have expertise based on practical knowledge, offered as situated knowledge that might be useful but not necessarily accepted because of its universal applicability.

Within conversation, there is a more open atmosphere, a space where the agenda or purpose flows from the conversation itself rather than from some preestablished agenda or way of operating. Conversations can be more fluid and spontaneous because there is no predetermined agenda or protocol. Moreover, members of a conversation experience more freedom and responsibility as they choose what they are going to talk about.

Conversation takes place when parties to a conversation feel there is room to say what they want without prejudgment and that what they say will be listened to and accepted. While this may sound like basic Carl Rogers, we take this a little further, assuming that to facilitate clients' feeling the space and room to say what they want, we should enter the conversation without any predetermined normative ideas about human functioning and without a predetermined notion of what should happen in the session. A predetermined agenda would endanger our listening to clients and allowing the purpose of the meeting to emerge between us and them.

"CURIOUS WITH"

A disposition that allows us to facilitate allowing space to open up for the client to speak whatever s/he wants is *curious with*. Our first exposure to this concept was through the influence of Harlene Anderson and Harry Goolishian (1988). They proposed that a therapist adopt a *not-knowing* and a *non-expert* position. This means that a consultant does not assume any expert knowledge about what is good or right for the client; instead, s/he adopts a naive and inquiring position. This disposition allows the consultant to be open to listen to clients without a predetermined normative structure for evaluating what they say. This disposition also allows us and our thinking to be changed, so that we can remain curious, and permits us to think in terms of conversation rather than interview.

If one has a normative structure of what makes for a healthy individual, one will more than likely ask questions to further the goal of making an assessment of how healthy this person is. The same would be true in working in a family therapy orientation. If one is "curious with" the client, questions will be asked as they develop within the conversation and with respect to the other conversant.

While Anderson and Goolishian (1988) and Cecchin (1987) spoke of the concept of curiosity, we have added the preposition "with." We worried that people would interpret this concept as "curious about" and, as such, it would carry the same disposition as one would have in an interview. In other words, the curiosity would be about what the interviewer was interested in, not what story the interviewee wanted to tell or create. When we say "curious with," the implication is that we are not curious about something of strictly our own agenda but rather curious with the client about what is relevant to her or him. We are curious within the client's emerging agenda. The direction emerges between us.

When we speak of being "curious with" someone, we think of two activities: (1) hearing, listening, and acknowledging what the other has said, and (2) asking questions. Both of these activities are oriented to (a) having the client feel understood, taken seriously, and interested in, (b) the consultant's seeking to understand and, as we will discuss in the next chapter, (c) the consultant's furthering creative conversation.

HEARING, LISTENING, AND AFFIRMING

When we are in conversation with someone and being curious with her or him, we listen to what s/he is telling us. We mean strictly listening. At the same time, we may summarize what we think we have heard or repeat what we have heard. We do this to check the extent to which we have heard what the client wants us to have heard and to let the person know that we are interested and taking what s/he says seriously. This listening involves head nods, nonverbal expressions, and other signals understood to be signs that we are following the conversation and attempting to understand.

This is not necessarily the traditional understanding of empathic listening. We are not looking to reflect only what someone is feeling. Our intention is to have clients experience our being curious with them, our being interested in them, and their being understood and taken seriously. We are listening and attempting to acknowledge what the client is saying.

The function or goal of listening has always been twofold. On the one hand, helping professionals have listened in order to understand what the client was saying and to make sense of it in terms of the constructs they as helpers had brought to the relationship. On the other hand, the goal of listening has been for the client to feel understood and listened to. In the past, when helping professionals thought of sessions as interviews, they put priority on *their* understanding what the client was saying. They did this for the professional's need to assess and make sense of what the client was saying. Professionals assumed they understood the client when they could talk about what the client said in terms of the professional constructs they brought to the interview. For example, if a professional worked in a structural family therapy model (Minuchin, 1978), then the professional would attempt to understand the client family in terms of enmeshment, detachedness, and other major constructs of the approach. A professional in a different orientation would be attempting to understand the client or the client's situation in terms of the major constructs of that orientation. However, a professional's understanding does not necessarily equate with the client's feeling understood.

When we change to a conversation metaphor, we are suggesting a shift of priority. We place a higher priority on the client's feeling understood and taken seriously. As Miller, Duncan, and Hubble (1997) point out, clients frequently report that empathy can be just a sense that the consultant is struggling and trying to understand even if the consultant apparently does not.

By the client's feeling understood, we foster an open space for further inquiry. In the past, we assumed that if we felt that we understood what the client was saying, then the client would feel understood. While that is often true, we do not assume the client's feeling understood necessarily follows from our feeling that we understand. At the same time that we are suggesting a higher priority on the client's feeling understood, we assume that it is impossible to be a totally neutral listener. We too bring our sensitivities and constructs to the conversation; however, we attempt to be affirmative in our listening and to use constructs that will allow us to listen in an affirmative way. What we mean by affirmative listening is listening for what people want us to appreciate (whether good or bad, exciting or disappointing), hearing the positive in people's intentions, and hearing the sincerity of their efforts despite the outcomes. Here are some examples of what clients say, what we hear, and how we affirm.

Hearing, Listening to, and Affirming Concerns*

What we mean by listening and acknowledging concerns is very simply listening with a sympathetic ear and acknowledging the concern. We might share our reactions as well. There is no assumption on our part that having clients talk more about the concern will necessarily make them feel better.

An example is a client who comes in saying that she is separated from her husband and young daughter and that she needs to stop using cocaine in order to maintain contact with her daughter. As she was talking about her

---

*We have borrowed the term *concerns* from our colleague, Michael Banks. The term allows us to acknowledge what the clients tell us without our involving distinctions of complaint, problem, or solution.

desire to make this change, I asked what other changes she might be looking for.

CONSULTANT: Any other change you are looking for?

CLIENT: I just want to get back to a normal life, have my daughter back living with me, get back to work, and some kind of normal structure I haven't had for several months.

CONSULTANT: This is different for you, to be apart from your daughter?

CLIENT: (*with some anger in her voice toward her separated husband and bordering on tears*) Yes, it's different to be apart from my daughter, to be out of my home, and not to be working. You know in the last six months it's like everything is just completely changed.

CONSULTANT: Oh, (*sadly*) I'm sorry you are having to go through all that.

This consultant response acknowledges the client's frustration and sadness about this situation. If we assumed that the client's feelings needed to be clarified or expressed, we would then attempt to spell out all the feelings she could be experiencing. Here, however, we are working under the assumption that she wants to tell us about her concerns. Since we are not thinking that we have to change or deconstruct any of her concerns, we attempt merely to acknowledge her telling the story and reflect our reactions. In this case, a simple statement of sadness was considered appropriate. Very often we find that clients merely want to know that the consultant understands and is sympathetic. Once they experience that understanding and acknowledgment, they relax and the conversation moves toward what they want.

Hearing, Listening to, and Affirming Wants and Desires

In reexamining the act of listening, we have noticed some differences in our own listening over the past several years. At one time, we thought of ourselves as Carl Rogers reincarnate. We thought of our listening as basically hearing what the client said to us and then reflecting back in a neutral fashion whatever affect we heard between the lines of what the client said. This was in keeping with the idea that reflecting clients' emotions would facilitate further expression of their emotions, which we assumed to be helpful. We also assumed that by our reflecting their emotions, they might begin to experience more congruence between what they were thinking or saying and what they were feeling. While we were doing that and attempting to show unconditional positive regard in the Rogerian mode, we were unaware of how much our hearing and, therefore, our listening were affected by our problem-oriented and pathology-oriented thinking.

If we were to assume that clients' problems or symptoms were caused or maintained by an incongruence between what they thought and how they felt, then this incongruence would be what we heard in what the clients said and what we listened for. If we were to assume that clients came to see us because of problems, symptoms, and pathology, then that would be what we heard and what we empathized with.

An example would be a man who came in and stated his distress about recent setbacks in his life. The conversation went something like this:

CONSULTANT: So, what are you coming in about?

CLIENT: Man, I do not know where to start. My wife has just informed me that she wants me out of the house by the end of this month. I knew things were bad, but I had no idea she felt this way. She won't even consider a second chance or going to counseling. She wants me out. I have tried to talk her out of it. She won't even think about it. On top of that she's turned my kids against me. They won't even listen to me.

Things can't go on like this. I don't know what to do. I gotta do something.

In the past, with our more problem orientation, we would have said to this man something like this: "It sounds to me that this has been very depressing and you're feeling rather overwhelmed." While we think this client would have felt understood and listened to, we surmise that only part of the story or only one possible story was heard and reflected back to him. With an exclusively problem orientation, only the problem part of the story was heard and only that part was reflected. What was not heard at that time was what this man might have been beginning to say about what he wanted. Today, we would be more sensitive to beginning statements of what he may be wanting.

An alternative reflection might go more like this:

CONSULTANT: It sounds to me that this has been very upsetting and shocking to you because you care a great deal about your family. On top of that, it sounds like you're quite anxious for some change.

What was heard differently and, therefore, reflected differently? In the first instance, depression and helplessness were heard and reflected. While these reflections may be true and fitting for the client, there may be more. By using the word "overwhelmed," we have perhaps closed down the discussion. The word leaves very few options for change and in response the client is likely to expand more on how overwhelmed he feels.

The second option reflects not only his feeling upset, but also his desire for change. The desire for change is more open toward the future than "overwhelmed." While both may be reflected and may be true for him, one closes the conversation down about possibilities in the future while the other possibly opens up hope.

What we are suggesting here is not that all reflective listening be turned upside down, from a problem orientation to a positive orientation. Being exclusively negative or exclusively positive can seem equally invalidating for the client. Clients are telling us what they want, what they are longing for, what changes they are looking for—and we can reflect that. The client will feel heard and validated and will probably expand even more on the desire.

Generally, if we offer two or more reflections to a client, s/he will respond to all of them but expand upon the last one heard. In other words, if we reflect in the above situation that the recent events have been upsetting and he seems to be anxious for some change, the client will hear both items. He will hear "upset" and he will hear "anxious for some change." What he will respond to and expand upon is the last one. So, we try to listen for what clients may be saying about their situation as well as what they want. We then try to use a language that opens up space for further conversation and perhaps for client hope. While this may sound like a positive relabeling, we do not think of it that way. The reflections flow from an assumption that people are attempting to communicate to us not only the story of their concern but also their desires and wants.

Another example is a woman who came to me with concerns about severe and disabling pain. When we initiated the first meeting, she began to tell me a heart-wrenching story of increasing pain. She told how the pain started in her hip over a year earlier. She went to the doctor, who tried different medications and suggestions for rehabilitation. The medications did not seem to help and the rehab exercises only hurt more. The doctor tried cortisone, which did not relieve the pain and instead triggered diabetes. This meant that she not only did not get relief but now she had to take insulin as well. She then began to get pain in her other hip. She could not work. When she came to see me she was also experiencing pain in her shoulder. Since she could not work and her husband's business was doing poorly, she had no health insurance. As she concluded her summary of her situation, I asked, "How are you hoping I may be able to help you with this?" She said, "I don't know. . . . All I know is, if I don't get things straightened out here, I'm going to kill myself."

Most of us would only hear this as a statement of desperation, as a statement of suicidal ideation. While not denying that, we hear something else as well, a beginning statement of what she desires, of what she may want. She may also be saying that what she wants is to "get things straightened out."

If we reflect only her thinking of killing herself, then this is what she hears from us as the meaning of her statement. If we assume that to a large extent people assume the meaning of their statement is how they perceive other people hear it, then what she might assume to be the meaning of her statement is a desire to kill herself. If, on the other hand, we reflect that it sounds like she is wanting to "get things straightened out," she may hear that as what I heard, and then expand upon it.

Hearing, Listening to, and Affirming Success

Another aspect of expanding our listening is not only listening for and hearing what people desire or want, but also for the times of success, when things go better or when they may feel more agency in their lives. In the same example, the woman responded to the reflection, "So, you want to get things straightened out?" with this statement. "I always used to be busy, doing things. Now it's an effort just to cook dinner."

In the past, we might have heard this statement as one more piece of evidence showing how overwhelming this woman's circumstances are. As listeners, we would have been feeling overwhelmed and wondering how we could possibly help this woman or how these circumstances could be changed. Now, we hear the horrible circumstances but also something different. The difficulty of the circumstances makes us that much more curious about how this woman is able to do anything at all, much less cook dinner. Given the circumstances, how is she able to do anything? Why hasn't she given up? So what comes to the foreground is not so much the circumstances, but the fact that despite those circumstances, this woman is cooking dinner.

From this position, I asked, "So, despite the circumstances, you cook dinner. There is no pain at that time?"

"No," she said, "There's pain, but I can do it for an hour or so."

"Still, it sounds like it must be very difficult. How do you manage to go that long?"

"I can do it."

We would like to point out that how you listen, and what you reflect to a client, are not neutral. What we hear and what we reflect emerge from our orientations, as well as the immediate content and relationship with the client. Given that clients tell us the stories that they see as relevant to be told, there are many stories that we can hear and reflect. We could hear a story of terrible circumstances of pain and of her being not only oppressed but also being overwhelmed by these circumstances. We could reflect this and inquire with her about the overwhelmingness of the situation. We could hear a story of courage and capability despite these circumstances, and we could further inquire about that.

These are not the only stories to be heard or the only stories to be inquired about. There are many, varied stories that could be told and further created. No one story is more accurate or in itself better. Some might conclude that the problem story is preferred. They might be operating under the view that true empathy comes from listening for the client's pain. Others might conclude that the more positive story is preferred. They might be operating from the view that positive talk is more likely to lead to solutions.

Our view is that neither problem conversation nor positive conversation is necessarily any better. While we hear both the pain and the courage, what seems most important is for the client to feel both that we are attempting to understand and that s/he is understood. If our own orientation dictates that we hear only problems or that we hear only solutions, there is the greater risk that our clients will not feel understood. Even more than our understanding the client, we want the client to feel understood and to feel that there is ample opportunity to say more of what s/he wants to say.

Hearing Differences and Acts of Courage

When we listen to our clients with a sensitive ear toward wants and positives, we are struck by clients' efforts and small acts of courage. We believe that, for the most part, our clients are well intentioned and really want the best for themselves and others. When we do not believe that they have sinister motives or are gaining something through their problem, we hear what they would tell us about themselves. What they most often tell us is that they do not want their problems and that, given the circumstances, they are trying their best. If we listen to our clients' stated intentions, we are often impressed with their courage.

An example is a woman who came to see us. When asked initially what she wanted from coming to the consultation, she said that she was an alcoholic and that she needed to stop. She said drinking was ruining her life, her health, and her marriage. She said that things were so bad that recently she threw her husband out. I asked if that was different. She said, "Oh yes." She then went on to say how there had been a lot of screaming and yelling and that it had become too much.

Later the client stated, "But I have gone back to work." I inquired, "How did you take the risk to go back to work?" Because of the context, I saw this decision "to go back to work" as an act of change and courage. Again, this is not a positive relabeling or an attempt to boost this woman's self-esteem. I used this language because I heard it as a risky thing to do and therefore saw the woman's action as an act of courage.

A strategic orientation would be to take an action that is seen by the client as negative and turn it into a positive, with the intention of boosting self-esteem or enabling the client to see herself as having the capability to take on more actions. The reframe would have the intention of leading to the pragmatic consequence of a different attempted solution, as well as more action on the client's part. Within a personal consultation approach, we have no such strategy in mind. However, as we pay attention to the circumstances and what clients are telling us within their intentions and view of what they are attempting to do, they appear more valiant and good hearted.

Hearing Preferred Intentions and Preferred Views of Self

We became more aware of the usefulness of the concept *preferred view of self* through reading the work of Joseph Eron and Thomas Lund (1996). They have written about how in problem stories clients often feel that their preferred view of themselves may not be shared by others or may be in conflict with how others view them. What we have found useful about this idea is that clients appear to feel increasingly validated and tend to expand more about themselves when they perceive us as understanding and appreciating their preferred view.

Here is an example from a training tape. The client is an airline mechanic who has been ordered to come to counseling as a condition of his probation from his job.*

CONSULTANT: What are you wanting from coming here?

CLIENT: I was told to come here (*sounding a bit sarcastic*). I was *ordered* to come here if I want to keep my job. I was a victim of random drug screening. They found evidence of marijuana in my urine.

This was a surprise to me, cuz I wasn't smoking on the job. I mean, I don't know how much you have to smoke to have it show up in your urine. I just never imagined that what I do at home could have any bearing on what I do at work.

CONSULTANT: So, this is not the sort of thing you would normally do. You wouldn't do this if you thought it would jeopardize your performance on the job. It's a surprise to you.

CLIENT: Right! No, no, I would never smoke on the job.

What I hear from the client in this story is that all this seems very unfair. He has been ordered to come to counseling for something he does not think is wrong. Further, he seems outraged that he is being accused of being irresponsible on the job and jeopardizing his position. His preferred view of himself seems to be a responsible employee who would never do anything to negatively affect his performance. To his way of thinking, this is why he does not smoke marijuana before or during his work hours.

As I support this preferred view of himself, I am hoping that I have understood what he is wanting me to know about him and that he feels not only understood but also appreciated for his preferred view and his good intentions. With this apparent acknowledgment of his good intentions, the conversation becomes more open and we can begin to discuss what, if anything, *he* wants from coming to the consultation. The advantage for the conversation, and for the client, is that generally when clients hear some acknowledgment of their view of themselves or their intentions, they relax from the fear of judgment. With this relaxation, the conversation opens even more and clients feel free to expand within the conversation.

Our intention here is not to suggest that all listening should be for positives or that all clients might have good hearts and good intentions. However, by acknowledging to ourselves that our attempting to understand events from the client's view is more useful than trying to interpret what they may mean to us, we will hear stories differently. Whatever we reflect to the client, the client responds to. If our reflections to the client are validating in some way, the conversation opens up even more.

---

*This training tape is entitled *Working with the mandated client: A solution-focused interview with John Walter.* The tape is produced by Master'sWork Video Productions of Los Angeles, directed by Jennifer Andrews and David Clark.

QUESTIONS ARISING FROM BEING "CURIOUS WITH"

Above we described how being "curious with" involved two activities. The first is hearing, listening, and acknowledging, and the second is asking questions. Questions are asked to let clients know of our interest in what they want to tell us, to let the clients experience our attempting to understand, and to further a creative conversation. Clients know we are interested in what they want to tell us when we listen attentively. They also know that we are interested and curious when we ask relevant questions.

When we used to do diagnostic interviews and follow strict interview protocols, clients would frequently look at us with an expression that said, "Why are you asking that question?" The question seemed too far afield from what they were coming in about or the preceding conversation. Now, in our desire to enable clients to feel understood and to take seriously their wanting something from coming to see us, we ask questions that arise within the conversation and are relevant to their purpose in coming to see us. Therefore, questions arise from listening and from the content and process at hand.

In the following chapters, we will discuss how some questions can be useful in creative conversations. The suggested questions do not determine the course of the consultation, however. The conversation determines when and if a question may be relevant or useful.

Curiosity and wonder are facilitated when we ask questions without an end in mind. When we used strategic approaches we asked questions in order to get a client to some place. We would overstate our pessimism in order to get the client to be more optimistic. We would imitate the bumbling one-downness of TV detective Columbo in order to get the client to explain more. We would caution people against change in order to free them to change.

Our questions are not designed to get clients to talk in a different way or to talk about something that we think they should talk about. While we have some questions and distinctions that we think can be helpful, we do not have an answer in mind. For example, while we think it can be helpful to talk with a couple about what they want from coming to see us, we are not experts about what they should want or how their marriage should be. We assume an expertise about how to facilitate a creative conversation, not what the content should be.

Let us now shift our attention to the asking of questions in order to further a creative conversation. We will now discuss the mutual creating of preferences and possibilities.

CHAPTER FIVE

Inquiring of Desire
From Goals to Preferencing

Historically, therapy has been about treating the structure underlying the presenting problem and thereby healing the structure or fixing the problem. With the arrival of solution-focused approaches, the business of therapy became the constructing of a solution. While the focus shifted to the future and to solutions, the assumptions remained within a problem/solution configuration.

In place of this configuration we are suggesting something different. We assume that when clients come to see us they are coming because they *want* something, they desire some change as a result of their coming. This assuming that clients want something from coming to see us has led us in a different direction.

In place of the problem/solution distinction or the deficit/strength distinction, we focus on preferencing. If one subscribes to or uses the problem/solution distinction, one begins to create stories of the problem and/or stories of the solution. In a problem-solving orientation, one assumes that a client comes in seeking a solution to a problem. One first looks for the underlying cause of the problem or the interactional pattern of the problem before one begins to consider what might be a solution. Usually, problem-solving orientations are built upon spatial-temporal metaphors. The problem is conceptualized as existing as a concrete reality in the present. The solution is conceptualized as a concrete state as well but existing in the future. The two states exist as distinct states that are separated by space and time. The task of problem-solving therapies is to somehow create the transition from one state to another, to get the client from the problem state to the solution state.

Problem state or present state ———→ Solution state in the future

Problem-solving orientations assume that making this transition requires some doing on the client's part or perhaps on the therapist's part. To the extent that the transition is conceived as the client's doing, the first action is to break down this "doing" into smaller, more manageable steps. This parceling intervention is seen as necessary because the client is commonly thought of as overwhelmed by the problem and perhaps experiencing feelings of low self-worth. When the problem is broken down into small, manageable steps, the client's actions are more possible and probable. The word *steps* indicates movement within the spatial metaphor over time. To get from one state to another requires either client action or therapist intervention or both.

The problem/solution distinction creates different courses of action within narrative or poststructural therapies. The distinction has given rise to the organization of whole orientations around one side of the distinction or the other. Problem-focused brief strategic therapy (Weakland et al., 1974) focuses on breaking up the interactional pattern of the problem and attempted solution. Solution-focused brief therapy (de Shazer et al., 1986; O'Hanlon & Weiner-Davis, 1989; Walter & Peller, 1992) is organized around solution-construction processes.

The narrative approach and practices (Freedman & Combs, 1996; Parry & Doan, 1994; White & Epston, 1990; Zimmerman & Dickerson, 1996) have described the deconstruction of the problem and the creation of preferred realities. At the same time, the collaborative language systems approach (Anderson, 1997; Anderson & Goolishian, 1988) has assumed that clients come in because they sense a lack of personal agency with regard to some life situation. The collaborative language systems approach assumes that the problem exists within the language that clients are using in order to make sense of the situation. If the problem exists and is maintained within language, then by engaging in dialogue and deconstructing that language, the problem will not necessarily be solved but it will dissolve.

The deficit/strength distinction creates other courses of action. If one works under this distinction, the first course of action is to make some assessment of deficits. The assessment of deficits directs a therapist to interventions or resources to fill in or address the deficits. The strength model (Rapp, 1998) or perspective (Saleebey, 1992) directs a therapist to assess for strengths in the individual or family. This assessment enables the therapist to see the client as more capable and to facilitate the utilization of the strengths.

Given our orientation to desires and preferences, we have decided to abandon the problem/solution distinction (structural, poststructural, or narrative) and the structural distinction of deficits/strengths or pathology/health. With the distinction of preferences, our work focuses on the creative aspects of conversing. We assume that our conversations are going to be about desires, wants, or preferences. In conversation language, the distinction of preference becomes preferencing.

In adopting the language of preferencing and conversing, we are also moving away from spatial-temporal metaphors and linear thinking. As we indicated above, problem-solving approaches assume a present state and a future, problem-solved state. The goal of therapy is to make the transition from one state to the other through some action or intervention.

We see preferences as a centerless web of possible desires with no one desire being necessarily a means to another. Personal consultation becomes conversing about these possible desires. As clients converse about what they want, a new language evolves that allows them to recognize what they want as already occurring in their life or that allows different actions that did not seem available before.

We believe that clients come in with some sense of desire and that asking them about that desire is a good place to start.

CONCERNS AND SITUATIONS

While we may begin the meeting by asking clients what they want from coming in to see us, we find that many people want to share with us their concerns about their present situation first. Many people seem to find it helpful to express all their concerns, either to get their feelings about their situation off their chest or to get the chance to make their concerns public and have someone else understand. While in our solution-focused past we may have discounted clients' telling of their concerns because of our zeal to get to the "real" stuff of constructing solutions, we are no longer in such a rush. No conversation is truly mutual if we are pushing for an agenda to move out of talking about concerns. Clients tell us that it is very important for them to have the feeling that we are concerned and that they are understood.

We have also found that some clients want to share with us their present experience or situation. After sharing their concerns most clients indicate some desire to move on to what they want. We generally summarize what we have heard, perhaps express some support about it, and then, if the conversation indicates, invite a conversation about what they want from coming to see us. This is the beginning of having the purpose emerge between us. Asking, "What do you want from coming *here*?" insures that purpose will emerge that is relevant to our meeting.

Here is an example from the opening of a first meeting.

CONSULTANT: (*after having explained the way we work and what to expect*)
Can you tell me what you are wanting from coming here?

CLIENT: Well, (*sigh*) I'm married. I have a daughter who is two years old. (*She smiles*.)

CONSULTANT: Ahh, a delightful age.

CLIENT: Yes, it is. But, the reason I am here is because lately I've been feeling a lot of stress at work and at home.

A lot of things have come up from my childhood that did not bother me until now. It may have bothered me then but I never brought it up or touched the subject. But now that I'm seeing my daughter growing up and how wonderful that is, all these things have been coming up as far as my parents.

I come from a small family with three kids and I am the middle child. My parents divorced and at the time that didn't affect me as much as now.

Since my daughter is my first child, I want to do the best for her and the best that I can give her. But sometimes between work and home, it is not the best. A lot of things come up about my parents. I have always thought that I come from a dysfunctional family. My father was abusive to my mother and sometimes to us the kids too. We just sort of accepted it at the time, but we never had my father there.

She describes further how today her extended family is scattered all over the country and even when they get together they are not very close or united. She finds this disappointing, since she would like her daughter to feel connected to her grandmother and the whole family, but there seems to be such emotional distance.

CLIENT: At work, with some of the people I work with I have to watch behind my back. If I or anybody makes one mistake, there is always someone trying to show you up. So, there is just a lot of pressure there too.

Physically, I am going through a lot and so I went to my doctor. She said, "What is really going on with you? You are young and have all these symptoms." So, she said that maybe it would be good for me to go see someone. So . . .

With this concluding statement, her voice drops, her hands drop some and she looks to the consultant as if to say, "So that's it." She appears to be looking for the consultant to respond or take the lead at that point.

At this point, we assume that she is inviting us to respond and/or perhaps take the lead. We could acknowledge what she has said and invite further exploration or a different direction by asking a question. If she appears to want to talk more about her concern, then that is what we do. We may ask if there is more about her concern that she would like us to know or if she would like to describe for us what she wants or how she would like things to be.

To acknowledge what she has said, we could say, "Sounds like there is a lot going on for you that is creating quite a lot of stress. Sounds also like you are looking for some changes for yourself. Could you say, then, what you are hoping for from coming here?" This question invites a discussion of purpose, of what she wants from coming to the consultation. What she has described so far sounds like a beginning description of her situation. However, at some point, when the conversation lends itself, we want to begin an inquiry about what she wants from coming to see us. We want to begin a conversation of preferences and purpose.

There exists a danger that we could assume to know what she wants by interpreting her situation. We could assume that she wants help with stress, or with parenting, or with her relationship, or with issues arising from how she was parented. We want to avoid assuming what she wants. So, we are very deliberate and straightforward about asking not just what she wants, but, more to the point, what she wants from our meeting. In other words, while a husband might *wish* to keep his marriage together, when asked *what he wants from coming to see us*, he might say that he wants help separating. We are distinguishing what clients might want in their lives from what they might want as the result of coming to see us. Asking clients what they want from coming to see us insures that we as consultants do not jump to conclusions about what clients want and initiates a conversation about the purpose of the consultation.

As we write this, we are aware that our talking about preferencing sounds almost prescriptive, as if we are suggesting that you have to get the client to talk about what s/he wants as a goal. This is not the case. If a client wants to talk about her or his concerns, that is what s/he wants. It is not up to us to stop that conversation. What we have found, however, is that, as clients talk about their concerns, they are already hinting at or beginning to say what they want. If we assume that their concern is what they do *not* want, they may already be talking about what they *do* want. Talking about what they *do* want becomes a conversational transition from discussing concerns to discussing what they want from coming to consultation.

WHO WANTS WHAT?

As we mentioned before in the chapter on inspiring inquiries, we assume that the customer for our service becomes obvious as we ask ourselves, "Who wants what from coming to see us?" We keep this question in mind throughout the first meeting and whatever following meetings there may be. The answer may change from meeting to meeting.

While in some cases an entire family may come in, it may become apparent that not all of them are concerned about the situation or want something to be different. Perhaps only the mother is concerned about her teenager. The younger children, while they are affected by the problem, may see themselves as not nearly as concerned as mother about the teenage son's dropping grades and recent troubles with the police. The stepfather, while concerned, may have washed his hands of the situation and therefore not be interested in participating. At the same time, there may be a probation officer who has become involved and is responsible to the court for the decision or recommendation of when to terminate the probation.

For every meeting, we listen for or ask directly,

What do you want from coming here?

We ask this question of everybody who indicates some interest in the situation. With a family that came in, the conversation went like this:

CONSULTANT: So, what are you wanting from coming here?

The family consists of a 15-year-old girl, an 18-year-old girl who was not there, and the parents. As I asked this question, they all looked at one another and then mother nudged the 15-year-old to speak.

DAUGHTER: I would like things to be better, but he needs to stop bitching (*pointing at her father*). He can't seem to stop. He bitches about everything. If it's not done perfectly, it's not right. My sister is perfect, I'm the bad kid. I get along with my mother, but I feel bad that she is in the middle.

CONSULTANT: Hmm. So, you would like things different between you and your dad. You think he wants things different as well?

DAUGHTER: He doesn't try. I go halfway but he always messes things up. He keeps trying to get into my business. He listens to my phone calls. I want him to respect my business.

CONSULTANT: Tell me more about that last part.

DAUGHTER: I would like him to have a little more respect for me. He says, "How can I have respect for you when you don't respect me?"

CONSULTANT: This is true, you would like more respect between you? (*directed to father*)

FATHER: I would like her to respect me, but not just me. I would like her to respect herself.

CONSULTANT: How do you mean?

FATHER: I would like to see her respect her things, respect herself, and stay in school.

After the father had spoken more of how much he wanted her to stay in school and pass her subjects, I asked mother what she might want.

MOTHER: I would like to see the fighting stop. I am always in the middle trying to keep them apart. I honestly think that if I weren't there, something awful would happen.

In this beginning conversation, each one of them has begun to indicate that they want something from coming to the meeting. Later, they explained that the other daughter did not see this as her concern and was not coming.

When clients come to see us because they have been mandated to come in or someone else is urging them to come in, we find it useful to explore what the person mandating the consultation may want, in addition to what the client in front of us wants. In some situations we may have several clients, all with the same initially stated preferences or with different preferences. For example, the airline mechanic mentioned in the previous chapter came in because his employer had put him on probation after traces of marijuana showed up in a random drug screen. In this case the question of who wants what leads to several other questions, for instance: What does the client in front of us want? What does the client in front of us think his employer wants? What does his employer want?

What the client in front of us wants is paramount. S/he may want something strictly for her or himself. However, the client may want merely to fulfill the requirements of the mandate. This is a suitable place to start. Depending on what the client says he wants and what he says about his situation, we may decide to call his employer to find out if his employer wants something as well. If the employer wants something or is interested in the client's fulfilling certain requirements that the employer has indicated, then we have two clients—the employee coming in to see us and the employer who is ordering the consultation.

Here is the sample dialogue, including the portion mentioned in the previous chapter.

CONSULTANT: (*describing how we work lets the client know what to expect*)
So, let me explain to you how I work so that you know what to expect. I would like to talk with you for about 45 minutes about what you might be hoping for from coming here, what changes you may be looking for, and anything else you might want to tell me. Then, I would like to take a short break, during which I will go in the other room for a couple minutes to think over what we have discussed. Then I will come back and share with you some of my thoughts and exchange with you any further thoughts or reactions you may have. Okay?

All right, can you tell me what you want from coming here?

CLIENT: I was *told* to come here (*sounding a bit sarcastic*). I was *ordered* to come here if I want to keep my job. I was a victim of random drug screening. They found evidence of marijuana in my urine.

This was a surprise to me, cuz I wasn't smoking on the job. I mean, I don't know how much you have to smoke to have it show up in your urine. I never imagined that what I do at home could have any bearing on what I do at work.

These comments by him I hear as his resentment that he has been accused of something wrong and that he has been ordered to come here. At the same time it seems that he sees himself as a responsible employee who would not be smoking pot if he thought that it would affect his job. So, this is what I attempt to reflect and hope that he finds it validating.

CONSULTANT: So, this is not the sort of thing you would normally do. You wouldn't do this if you thought it would jeopardize your performance on the job. It's not something you do on the job. This is a surprise to you.

CLIENT: Right! No, no, I would never smoke on the job. (*His reaction seems to indicate that he feels that I have heard his own sense of responsibility.*)

CONSULTANT: I take it you would like to keep your job. (*I am curious if this may be what he is wanting from coming to see me. He says that he likes this job very much and that it is a very good job. He also states that he does his job very well and his good job ratings are part of his surprise about his boss's complaint. I offer this further supportive and clarifying statement.*) So, coming here wasn't your idea, but given the options you decided to come in.

CLIENT: Yeah (*with a nod and smile*).

CONSULTANT: Anything more they told you? (*I am curious, given that he prefers to keep his job, what else his employer may have told him he has to do in order to keep his job. I am also beginning to get the impression that another client here is his employer.*)

CLIENT: They made it clear my job is at stake and that they are looking out for my best interests. I don't know what they mean by that (*with a bit of sarcasm*).

CONSULTANT: So, what's your best guess of what it is that they are looking for from your coming here?

CLIENT: I don't know. I think they are wanting me to quit smoking pot. (*With a somewhat angry tone*) I don't know what is going on. It kinda makes me paranoid. I never know when they might be handing me a cup. I mean, I had no idea it would affect me at work. So, now they are in my life in a way I don't appreciate.

CONSULTANT: Yeah! So, what are your thoughts of what you have to do according to your boss in order to keep you job?

CLIENT: Well, I guess, I have to see you. I have to get a report and I sort of have to stop smoking pot.

And I guess, if all goes well, I'll keep my job.

A preference seems to be emerging here that he wants to keep his job. His impression of what his employer, the other potential client, may want is his coming to counseling, his stopping marijuana use, and his obtaining some report. What I am curious about, in keeping with our "Who wants what?" question, is: what all his employer may be wanting from his coming here, what his employer may want in the report, if my client wants to do these things in order to keep his job, and how he may be hoping I may be able to help.

CONSULTANT: Anything more they are saying or that you are thinking you have to do?

CLIENT: It looks like I am being told to stop smoking pot. Now it's been a week since I've smoked but I don't know if I want to quit, or if I can quit, or if it's right that they should make me quit.

In hindsight, I find myself curious about his saying he is not sure that he can quit. Does his doubt about his ability to quit in some way have relevance to his decision whether to quit? If he thought he could quit, how might that make a difference to him? Would he be more inclined to quit if he thought he could? I wish I had asked those questions, as they might have opened the conversation even more. Instead I offered a reflection of his sense of being wronged.

CONSULTANT: Seems unfair to you.
CLIENT: Yeah, I do my job very well.

He expands on his feeling wronged and how this is not making him more loyal to the company. After his talking about his reaction, I am curious about something else he mentioned. Given his possible desire to quit smoking pot in order to keep his job, I am curious about his offhand remark that he has gone several days without smoking pot.

CONSULTANT: I am struck by something. You haven't smoked in a week. How'd you do that?
CLIENT: Well, they've got me kind of worried. I'm rattled. But I don't smoke that often anyway. I just resent that I can't.

The discussion of the week without smoking does not seem to have relevance to him in terms of his thinking any more positively about his being able to quit and so I move on. I suggest to him that maybe it would be helpful to talk about his quitting and what would be signs that he was making progress. The conversation seems flat, and in hindsight I suspect it was flat because he had not really decided for sure that he wanted to quit or that quitting was what he wanted from coming to see me. So, I reflect that.

CONSULTANT: Sounds like you haven't figured out what you want to do yet. You're going along for now because you want to keep your job. But it sounds like you're not sure what you want to do or what would be worth it to do.
CLIENT: Right.
CONSULTANT: (*I follow up on one of the other requirements, the report.*) So, in terms of this report you mentioned that they want from today, would it be helpful for them to know you haven't smoked in a week?
CLIENT: Yeah, but it's really the drug screens. The thing is, I think they are just covering their butts.
CONSULTANT: So, the screens are the ticket for you.
CLIENT: Yeah, and the report's showing a willingness to work on the problem.
CONSULTANT: So, if we were to write out this report for today, which is usually the way I do it, which is to write the report together, what would we put down that would be evidence of your willingness to work on the problem?
CLIENT: My coming here and talking with you.

Consultant: (*A little later in the conversation. We have talked about his impression of what his employer wants and about his liking his job. I am curious still what he wants from coming to see me.*) So, this may sound like a strange question, given that we are near the end of our meeting, but is there something about all this that I can help *you* with?

CLIENT: Well, I don't know if I can quit. I've been smoking a long time. It's such a part of my life. I'm going to have to make a decision soon and I think if I have to stop smoking, I'm going to need some pointers. I don't know if you understand I can barely imagine my life that way.

CONSULTANT: Hmm.

CLIENT: I don't know if I can work somewhere else and not have the same problem. I'm checking that out. So, I don't know if there is much point in my talking about my quitting yet.

Have you been able to help other people quit?

CONSULTANT: Yes, I have helped some people.

We have begun a conversation with an evolving sense of purpose. He has indicated that he likes his job, he resents that he has been unfairly accused of wrongdoing and required to see me, and that he is unsure yet of what he wants to do. He may quit pot in order to save his job, but he is not sure that he wants to do that or that he could do that. He needs this initial report that we will write up. This I reflected to him and asked if he would like to set another appointment or if he would like to think about it. He indicated that he would like to think about it.

He has indicated that his employer has set certain requirements for him to keep his job. I ask his permission to contact his employer in order to check on these requirements and to see if I have another client.

` The employer may take the position that they have stipulated the conditions in order for him to keep his job and that is all they want. They are offering counseling as a benefit of his employee assistance package, but this is just a procedure that they have to follow. They may want the reports just to verify that he is using consultation and want no further contact with me other than to check that procedures are being followed.

On the other hand, the employer may want to talk with me and be interested in helping this employee make the best of the situation. In this case, I would work with them as a client as well. I would ask them what they want from his coming to see me and how I might be able to help them. The conversation could go like this:

CONSULTANT: I saw your employee yesterday and received his permission for me to talk with you. I just first wanted to check with you about what you were hoping for from sending him to me.

EMPLOYER: Well, I'd like to see him turn this around. I don't know how long he's been into drugs, but his record has been very good until now. I'd like to help him if I could.

CONSULTANT: What makes you want to see him turn this around and keep him as an employee?

EMPLOYER: Well, he's had an excellent record and gets along with everyone in his area very well. If the evidence hadn't shown up in the screen, we would not have had any idea from his job performance that there was any problem.

CONSULTANT: So, you value his teamwork and his performance. Besides his results on the screens, is there anything else that would tell you that he was turning this around?

EMPLOYER: Well, if his attitude around all this was cooperative. Lately, he's been very belligerent.

Here is an indication that she is interested in change in the situation. The conversation would continue in this preferencing fashion.

In terms of our "Who wants what?" at this point, the employee has indicated some interest but is not committed to further meetings. If the employer indicated interest in his changing and her wanting to be involved, then we would engage in conversations like the one above either on the phone or in person.

When the employee called and came in for a second appointment, the "Who wants what?" question was still relevant.

CONSULTANT: So, what would you like from today?

CLIENT: I think I want to keep my job.

CONSULTANT: Yeah, you want to keep it?

CLIENT: Yeah, but I'm actually a little scared. I smoke to relax. So, if I am not smoking, then I'm not relaxed. I don't enjoy drinking.

CONSULTANT: So you are concerned about that.

CLIENT: Yeah.

CONSULTANT: How'd you decide to keep your job and come here?

CLIENT: I know it's not going to be any different anywhere else. I got bills, credit card payments. I just gotta deal with it.

CONSULTANT: Sort of bite the bullet?

CLIENT: Yeah! I am not happy about it. In fact, I am quite pissed. This past week I just put my hand through a wall. Then, I smoked.
    I am a nice guy when I smoke.

CONSULTANT: You mean you are not a nice guy when you don't?

CLIENT: I am a nice guy but stuff builds up. Smoking relieves the stress. Now, I am not sleeping.

CONSULTANT: To say the least, you are not pleased about the choice you are having to make.

CLIENT: No! They are making my life a lot harder.

CONSULTANT: But at the same time, despite your concerns you have decided to keep your job and deal with it.

So, tell me, what would be some signs that you were dealing with it and keeping your job?

CLIENT: Well, I guess I wouldn't be thinking about it. There wouldn't be this tension and stress.

What is evolving between us is a sense of purpose in our conversation. He has decided to keep his job and to comply with the requirements of the company. He appears to see smoking marijuana as a means of dealing with the stress of his life and so beginning signs that things were going better would be that he would no longer be thinking of marijuana and he would feel less tension.

In terms of our assumption that the consultation group is formed within language, we ask, "Who wants what?" of ourselves. Our asking "who" helps us determine whom to talk to and who our clients are. Asking "what" begins a preferencing process, creating purpose or preferences within our meetings and perhaps beginning possibilities.

The conversations would continue to evolve with him around what he says he wants, that is, keeping his job, dealing with the situation, and dealing with the stress and tension. With his employer, the conversations would continue, probably by phone, about what she has stated she wants, which is to attempt to help him make the change.

A VISUALIZATION OR STORYING METAPHOR

A helpful metaphor for creative conversations is visualization. With this metaphor, we think of ourselves as engaging with clients in a process of creating movies or stories of how things will be when things are going the way they want. In a previous publication, we used an example from sports psychology and hypnosis to illustrate this metaphor:

A few years ago we were watching the Winter Olympics. In the bobsled event, we noticed the East German women as they were preparing for their run down the hill. As they were sitting in the sled waiting their turn, their eyes were closed. We thought this was rather strange. Then we noticed that with their eyes still closed, they were making strange weaving motions forward, backward, and side to side. We thought this really strange—until the commentator explained that these women were going through a mental preparation of the run. With their eyes closed, they were visualizing going through the run; their body movements were their body responses as they imagined banking off of turns and experiencing the acceleration of the run. (Walter & Peller, 1992, p. 11)

This visualization or hypnosis metaphor gives us a way of thinking about the conversation. We do not mean to take this example literally. We do not formally use hypnosis, visualization, or visual language. However, we imagine that we and our clients are conversationally constructing images, stories, or experiences where what they want in their life is happening, that is the preferences and possibilities they are seeking. Rather than imagining one visualization, we are creating many visualizations or stories. This metaphor gives some shape to our conversing and storying.

The advantage of the visualization metaphor is that it inspires some possible conversations or directions for what we are doing. It is not to be taken literally. It is a way of making sense of the constructive storying within language that is taking place. As we said before, this creative conversation can create preferences and alternatives.

As we will note in the examples, this visualization is not taken literally and it is not a first step in a problem-solving process. In other words, we are not attempting to create an image of the future to be followed by a discussion of how the client could make that image happen. We do not make images of a future as a brainstorming exercise before plotting out strategies of accomplishment. This metaphor is merely an heuristic device to open up the conversation, to create a story of desire, and to create a story that is outside of the problem/solution distinction. As we and the clients story about desire, a new language emerges. The consequences of this and how this works will be discussed further at the beginning of chapter seven.

While it may seem natural to think of this as creating a visualization of the future, we are talking about images or stories without a time frame. They are stories or images of what the client wants. The images probably seem to have a future tense about them because most of us think of our goals and desires as being in the future. However, when we talk about creating preferences, these constructs are just devices without a temporal reference. We may find that as the language develops around what clients want in their life, we and the clients find that some of what they want is already in their experience or that they now more easily identify it in the future.

In keeping with the visualization metaphor, we are more curious about what clients say they *do* want. While clients may speak of the problem or what they do not want, we invite them to talk more about what they do want. We learned from Erickson that it is impossible to make a picture or think of not doing something or of something not happening. We can only make pictures of something positively happening.

In order to make this concrete and real for yourself, try just for a moment or two *not* to allow yourself to think of a picture or hint of an image of a piece of chocolate cake. Our guess is that by now, as you attempt to do this, you are chuckling to yourself as you realize that it is already too late. By now you have already had the image or thought or taste of chocolate cake. What you will further discover is that, ironically, the more you try not to think of something, the more you think about it. So, again, if you were to try not to think of chocolate cake, the more you tried not to think of it, the more you would probably think of it. Each attempt to not think of it brings up a repeat image or another image of the chocolate cake.

This is the inadvertent drawback of approaches that focus exclusively on problems with no deconstruction or change of meaning. The more the conversation is drawn to talking of the problem, the more the client and therapist are thinking of and associating further about the problem.

The more a conversation is focused on not-drinking as a problem or as a preference, the more both client and consultant are thinking of drinking. The scenario becomes similar to this. A person wakes up in the morning and says to her/himself:

> I am not going to drink today. In fact, I am not even going to think about drinking. I am not going to think about that six pack I have out in the car. I am not going to think about having a few at lunch. I am not going to think about stopping off on the way home. I am not going to think about having a cocktail or two or more at dinner. I am not going to think about a nightcap. I am not even going to think about that bottle I have stashed so that no one else will find it.

What is this person thinking about all day? Drinking. Who of us, if we are thinking of something that we like that much, will have the willpower to say, "No"?

What makes more sense, both pragmatically and metaphorically, is to think of something else. What makes even more sense is to think of what we want to happen or what we want in our life rather than trying to stop thinking about or eradicating what we do not want.

If the client, who is complaining about drinking, begins to think of and talk of what s/he does want, the conversation moves to how s/he wants, for example, "a clear head and plans for what to accomplish that day." These images, "clear head" and "plans," are things that a person can begin to imagine and to direct attention to.

Our belief is that whatever clients call their attention to begins to happen more often. This happens in both positive and negative ways. We have all seen how parents who may be very vulnerable to the fear of their teens getting into drugs become hypervigilant for any signs of their teen becoming involved with drugs. Through the hypervigilance, both the parents' attention and the teens' attention are drawn to drugs. Soon, in many cases, the parents' worst fear takes place.

The opposite is also true. By shifting our attention and vigilance to what we want, the positive outcome we desire is more likely to happen. The practice of subliminal affirmation is an example of the focus on positive outcomes. A friend of ours would begin his day with a period of meditation. During this meditation, he would frequently repeat to himself the phrase, "Success is coming my way," or "I am good because I practice." The rationale of this meditation is that this message comes more to the fore of one's thinking and actions. If this message is present both subliminally and consciously, then one will notice more evidence of the message within one's day or one will take more actions consistent within the message.

So, we find it helpful to invite clients into conversations about what they *do* want. When we ask clients what they want from coming to see us, we are inviting them into a conversation in which we are mutually creating a movie of preferences. We invite clients to state in positive terms what they *do* want to happen in their lives and what they *do* want from coming to see us. While they may tell us what they do not want, we listen and acknowledge, and when the opportunity arises, we ask what they *do* want.

While we think creating stories, images, or experiences of what a client *does* want is important and helpful, the primary focus is on the conversation, that is, the listening and affirming of what the client is saying. Creating a positive image, description, or experience arises from within the conversation and is never forced. As a conversation continues, a consultant can do this in two ways: (1) by highlighting the desires within what the client is saying or (2) by directly asking what the client wants when the conversation provides the opportunity.

Highlighting Desires and Wants within the Conversation

A young woman came to see me and I started off asking her what she wanted from coming in.

CONSULTANT: So, what do you want from coming here?

CLIENT: (*with some urgency*) Gosh, where to start! I started work downtown about five months ago. It's really great. I live with my mom and I am from Peoria. I used to live with my father. I used to have this really close relationship with my father, but after this past weekend, I don't know if I really like him anymore.

There's so much going on. Now I am living with my mother and I feel like I am always getting hurt. It's emotionally stifling.

I just realized that if I want to move forward, I gotta deal with stuff.

Already, I am drawn into her story. I hear that she might want to be "moving forward" and "dealing with stuff." I am tempted to reflect these words and see if this is validating of what she wants from coming to see me. I could say, "So, you're wanting to be moving forward and dealing with stuff?" to which she might say yes and then expand.

However, there seems to be some urgency in her voice to tell me more of what she considers the whole story of what is going on for her. So, I mentally take note of what she may be wanting and decide to listen more to what she wants to tell me. I assume it is more important to her for me to understand than for me to push the conversation toward preferences. I assume that when she is satisfied that I have understood what she wants me to understand, then she will invite me to comment or ask a question.

This happens in everyday conversation as well. We assume a mutual interest and influence in the conversation. When I talk with someone, I assume that when I have said what I want my partner will ask a question, comment on what I have said, or share something related to our conversation. So here as well, going by the conversational rules of mutuality, I wait until she acknowledges that it is my turn. At this time in the conversation, I assume she wants to tell me more and that my turn will come.

CLIENT: I never allow myself to enjoy anything good that happens. It's like I don't deserve this. Something is going to go bad soon. Something is holding me back. I have only worked as a waitress or bartender.

But this new job is really great. I am working at a downtown hotel as the registration clerk. I feel like I have to be and look professional and—like a lot is being expected of me. People are looking at me. It is going really good.

Here I am tempted to ask how this new job is going so differently or how she is managing to enjoy this new job this far. This could lead to a conversation of difference or success. However, she seems still to want to tell me a whole story. So, I continue to just listen. (We will join that portion of the dialogue about her successes in chapter eight.)

She continues to tell me of events of this past weekend when she went to Washington, DC, for a family wedding. During this weekend, she found her father to be very controlling. He was telling her when to come home and warning her not to go partying with her cousin who is known to be into drugs.

She tells me how she was angry with her father and went off with her cousin anyway. Her cousin offered her some LSD and she took it. At the same party, her uncle fell while drunk and was screaming and blaming her along with everyone else. She said that blaming was typical of her father. Her father would always turn everything around so that he was the victim.

CLIENT: And that is what I do to myself. I turn everything around and sabotage stuff. Like, when I took the acid, I would say he gave it to me. It isn't my fault. But, I was the one who put it in my mouth. I knew exactly what I was doing. That is not the pattern I want to follow. I need to understand the situation and take responsibility.

CONSULTANT: (*I hear some conclusion in her voice and so I reflect what I hear she is wanting.*) That's what you would rather do—take more responsibility.

CLIENT: Yes, that is what I would like to be doing.

CONSULTANT: Tell me more about what you would rather have.

CLIENT: I would like to be taking responsibility for what I do good and what I do bad. Not sitting there placing blame on one thing or another.

This opening conversation has taken 25 minutes. I am hoping that she is experiencing me as listening to what she wants to say and taking it seriously.

I am hoping that she hears my interest, my curiosity, and my concern. I feel drawn into the story she is telling me and into her desire to be taking more responsibility.

My curiosity at this time is to hear more about this "taking responsibility," and so I might ask, "What makes you want to be doing that?" which invites her to describe further, and perhaps more strongly, her preference for this want at this time. Or I might ask her to tell me what the signs would be to her that she was taking responsibility. (The amplification of the preference and the creation of possibilities through "sign" language will be discussed in chapter seven.)

An alternative to listening and reflecting what we hear clients imply as their preferences is to ask directly. The woman mentioned earlier in the chapter came in concerned about the stress in her life, her desire to have the best for her daughter, and her longing to have both her family and work life be different. With her we would take the lead at the conclusion of her story to affirm what she had said about her situation and then directly set a direction by asking, "What do you want from coming here?" As we invite this direction in the conversation, we listen for and highlight what the client is saying that she *does* want, not merely what she wants to eliminate from her life.

An example of asking directly what the client wants, as opposed to highlighting what the client may want as s/he talks about her or his situation, involves a mother and small boy. When asked what they wanted from coming in to see me, mother stated very directly and specifically not only what the situation was, but also what she wanted.

CONSULTANT: So, tell me, what do you want from coming here, today?
MOTHER: Well, we have a problem. We have lots of arguments in the house. My boy seems to want to control the house.
CHILD: Yeah, I want my mom to move out. (*laughing and joking*)
MOTHER: He seems to think he should have things his way. So, he throws fits, he argues, and mouths off. The arguing really gets to me. He eventually does what he has to, even his homework. But by then I am frustrated and mad.

When meeting a family, we frequently ask soon in the conversation about times when the child is doing the right things. We find that children are much more likely to want to talk with us about the good times than the problem times. Sometimes, we find that children feel some relief that the consultant does not see them as bad and that we are just as curious about the good things they may be doing. Too often, we have found that after listening to parents talk about all the bad things their child is doing, the children are too embarrassed or too angry to want to talk with us. So, at this time I turn to him.

CONSULTANT: Is that right? Sometimes you do your homework?

CHILD: Yes, if it's easy.
CONSULTANT: How do you decide to do it?
CHILD: If it's easy and I know I can do it, then I do it.

Perhaps, he believes he only does the easy homework, but I am curious about and presume that there must be times that he does the hard homework as well. That would be even more impressive and perhaps leave him feeling more empowered.

CONSULTANT: Are there some times you do your homework even when it's hard?
CHILD: Sometimes, if I want to get it done so that I can do something else.
CONSULTANT: Really! Sounds like smart thinking. You do it so that you can do other stuff that you want to do. (*turning to mom*) Are there other things you are looking for from coming here?
MOTHER: I'd like him doing his homework, cleaning his room, taking a bath, brushing his teeth, and getting up on his own without my yelling.

The mother is beginning to describe what she wants from coming to the meeting. She has briefly described her concerns about the present situation. She has said that she is concerned about the arguments and her frustration with her boy. At the same time she has accepted the inquiry into what she wants from coming. She has specifically begun describing that she wants her young son to be doing, that is, several specific things without an argument.

This is the beginning of our creating purpose for our meeting. At this point in the session, I would be curious about how these changes by her son would make a difference to her. This inquiry, which we call "the significance of change," can sometimes open up the conversation more by expanding the overly focused language that she has used so far. She has said in very specific terms what she wants her son to be doing. As helpful as it might be to talk with her in specific terms about what she does want, we are also curious about how these things would make a difference to her. What would these changes by her son lead to for her?

She might say that, if he were doing these things on his own without her having to be after him, there would be more peace in the house, she would feel more relaxed with him, she would feel more relaxed with herself, and perhaps she would feel better about her boy. All of these expressions have the potential to open up the conversation both in a pragmatic sense and in emotional tone.

Pragmatically, focusing on the times when there is peace, when she is more relaxed with him or herself, and when she feels better about him might lead her to discover possibilities or options for her other than "being after him." For example, she might discover that when she relaxes herself, she is not quite as forceful or desperate in a way that sets him off into a power struggle. She might be firm but not heard by him as being critical.

Inquiring how this might make a difference for her also invites her to talk about what may be more important to her, which is to have good times with him. As she talks about what she wants in the sense of what is important to her about good times with him, the tone of the conversation can become less judgmental and more open. (More discussion of the possibilities that can arise by discussing the significance of change will take place in chapter six.)

In this meeting with the mother and son, we would also want to inquire about what her boy might want from the meeting. In keeping with our "Who wants what?" question, we would inquire at some point what he wanted. He might not want anything. Perhaps he came only because his mother insisted. He might want something now, or later in the conversation, or at a later meeting.

What he said was this:

CONSULTANT: Is there anything you would like from coming here today?
CHILD: No, not really.
CONSULTANT: (*inquiring a bit further*) There is nothing you would like to be different?
MOTHER: Isn't there anything you would like to learn?
CHILD: No, not really.
CONSULTANT: So, things are pretty cool for you. (*attempting to acknowledge what he said*) Is there anything you would like to be different between you and your mom?
CHILD: I'd like to play more games. She's always so busy or watching TV. When she screams at me she screams so loud.

This preference leads to a story of how he feels alone and bored after school and into the evening. This is followed by our storying a future of how he would like things to be, where he and his mother would be spending more time doing fun things, and how that would make a difference for him. This storying of what he wants and how things would be going according to his desires softens the tone of the meeting, as how much he values good times with his mother becomes obvious.

So far in the last chapter and this one, we have discussed the creating of a space for conversation and how we and the clients can begin a discussion of desires and preferences. We have discussed the importance of the question "Who wants what?" In the next chapter, we discuss another conversational tool that we have just mentioned—how exploring the significance of what clients want can open up the conversation even more.

CHAPTER SIX

Inquiring of the Significance of Change

From Means to Significance

Sometimes when clients state what they want from coming to see us, the language seems very confining and perhaps over-focused. We begin to feel confined within that language. Sometimes, what they want seems very much out of their control. They sometimes report that they have already tried many courses of action to bring about their desired change, with all their efforts leading to failure and frustration. What can facilitate the opening up of this language is the exploration of the significance of change, the significance of the achievement of their stated want. We explore this by asking about how the achievement of their preference would make a difference for them.

The question we ask most often to explore the significance of change is:

How would this change in _____ make a difference for you?

We fill in the blank with stated obstacles to change, their seemingly over-focused goals, desired changes in someone else, or changes in self or one's emotions that seem out of their control to change.

As we deconstruct this question, we see several presuppositions: We are presupposing that whatever change the consultant and client identify is going to make a difference. We are inviting the client into this same belief that the change s/he is talking about may make some difference. We are introducing the idea that what s/he is wanting could be thought of as a means to something else. The something else may open up the language and provide more possibilities for the client.

For example, in the previous chapter, the mother listed several things that she wanted her son to be doing. She wanted him to be doing his homework, taking a bath, cleaning his room, and brushing his teeth. All of these things might be very helpful for the young son to hear. Perhaps he has not before heard what his mother wants so specifically or in positive terms. At the same time, the conversation began to feel over-focused, as if she were struggling with him over these things. We can open up the conversation and the possibilities for her by asking, "Can you say how your son's doing these things might make a difference for you?"

The assumption here is that these changes by her son are going to make some difference to her. This difference may create more possibilities for both of them. She could say she would have more peace. Her having peace could lead to several things. She could find that she could get peace for herself in ways other than the way she is presently seeking. The way she is seeking peace now is by trying to get her son to do these things on his own. She might find that she can have peace when she does not try to accomplish quite so much in her day. She might have more peace when she relaxes her expectations of him or herself. She might find that when she is more at peace she approaches him differently. She might be less likely to struggle with him and instead state what she wants and walk away. He might find that his mother does not really mean to be yelling at him; she just wants some time to herself. He might find that, instead of her finding fault in him, she is beginning to see that he is more grown-up and capable. This might be something he can be proud of rather than struggling over with her. All of these are possibilities that may come up during discussion of what "peace" means to her. The notion of peace could open up this conversation for many preferences and possibilities.

The other presupposition we find within this question is that this change is going to make a difference *to the client*. We find that most often the client responds to this question by talking about herself rather than the other. In this example, the mother responds by talking about "peace" for herself. So, she shifts from talking about her boy to talking about what is important to her, which is having "peace" for herself. This leaves room for the other person, her son in this case, to be free to choose his own changes. He could see her requests as a way to help his mother have some "peace" rather than as something he is ordered to do.

We also find, as you will see in the following examples, that clients begin to speak more about themselves but very frequently in more personal and affective terms. This question seems to invite clients to talk about what is personally important to them. While the mother in this example is strong in expressing her desire for her son to be different, she is calmer as she discusses "peace" and what that would mean to her. Usually, as this happens, we find that as consultants we are drawn more into the conversation and the emerging story.

Using this question, "How would this make a difference to you?" introduces the distinction of means and ends into the conversation. The question proposes that this desired change be considered as a means to something else. It proposes that a change in someone else could be considered as a means toward something more important or at least toward something possibly within the client's control. By introducing this distinction, we propose another way of thinking and the possibility of creating a different kind of story in which the client can do something.

Let us go through some examples.

WANTING SOMEONE ELSE TO BE DIFFERENT

Recently, a young woman came in and said that she was quite upset by how a recent loss in her family had brought up some things that had never been resolved.

CLIENT: Recently, my sister died and in being at the funeral and around all my family I was just more aware of how my father has always been such a negative influence in my life. It's not that he ever told me not to do something or that I was stupid or crazy for doing something, but I just don't think he ever thought I could succeed.

CONSULTANT: How do you mean?

CLIENT: I don't know if he was jealous or just thought that women couldn't succeed, but he really did not want me to go to college. He just had such negative expectations. So, then I would doubt myself and what I wanted to do. When I expressed my doubts, my father never encouraged me to do it anyway.

CONSULTANT: You would like this to be different?

CLIENT: Yes, I really need to confront him about this. I wanted to at the funeral but I thought that was probably not the time to upset him and have this all out.

CONSULTANT: This is something you have done before?

CLIENT: No, not really. (*She says this rather sadly.*)

So far, she seems to be saying that these expectations and influences by her father have been holding her back. She also seems to be saying that she needs to get her father to admit or to stop these negative influences so that she, the client, would no longer feel held back and therefore could do something else. I am curious about how she thinks this change in her father *would make a difference to her.*

CONSULTANT: If your father were not this way, how would this make a difference to you?

CLIENT: I think I would be more adventurous. (*Her head picks up along with a slight rise in voice tone.*)

CONSULTANT: Adventurous! How do you mean?

"Adventurous" seems more personal to her and about her. I feel quite drawn into this and quite curious about how she would like to be. This may be possible to her without a change in her father and I am quite excited about this word *adventurous* and the possibilities it may open up. This new word gives both of us the opportunity to create a developing story of "adventurous."

CLIENT: Well, like lately I have been thinking I would like to try painting again.

CONSULTANT: This is different? What has you thinking of painting?

CLIENT: Well, nothing professional. But I used to do it when I was younger and my dad was always so critical. But now . . .

CONSULTANT: So, what makes you want to do it now?

CLIENT: I don't know. I just like that sort of thing.

CONSULTANT: How do you mean?

CLIENT: Well, like the last few years, I have taken this old house and totally restored it. It's an old turn-of-the-century house and my boyfriend and I have totally restored the frames, the woodwork, the colors, and the outside. It is really great. (*She says this with increasing excitement.*)

CONSULTANT: Now, how are you doing this? You could have told yourself that your father wouldn't have approved. (*This question invites an empowered storying, the creation of a story in which she is the principal character and in which she is doing what she wants.*)

CLIENT: I guess, but I guess there is this strong will in me.

CONSULTANT: Strong will? Tell me more about that.

CLIENT: Well, nobody in my family was artistic. But, I liked it, and so I would paint or dress up in different clothes and play-act sometimes even by myself when I was little.

The conversation begins with her stating that she feels held back by her father's negative expectations and she thinks she has to confront her father. As she talks of this her voice drops and she looks discouraged. The conversation seems to be constricting. We could conjecture that she sees a change in her father as necessary before she could get what she wants. As I asked *about how this change in her father would make a difference*, she says this change would lead to her being more "adventurous" and the tone of the conversation begins to change.

I think to myself *this* is what she wants, "to be more adventurous," and I inquire more about it. A story of preference seems to be emerging as she elaborates on what she means. She would like to be doing art, like she is doing now in restoring the house. She then amplifies the story by saying that she is doing this despite whatever negative influences because she has a strong will. A story is emerging now of her being strong willed.

These stories of preference are flowing one from another. While we could punctuate these stories and say that "adventurous" is the goal, we are not so sure that the labeling it as a goal is as important as the fact that these new stories are emerging. Both "adventurous" and "strong willed" seem like poignant themes or story lines that seem to give her more hope.

At the end of this meeting, I reflect to her how happy I am for her as I see her excitement about the refurbishing of the house and how intrigued and curious I am about this "strong will" that has survived and is still thriving. I encourage her to keep her eyes open for any times she notices that she is "adventurous" or "strong willed."

Another example is an elderly woman who complains about how her children never come to visit. She appears to feel somewhat powerless to make a difference for herself. She is bound to bed in a nursing home.

VISITING SOCIAL WORKER: How are you doing today?
CLIENT: Well, my kids didn't come over this weekend again. I don't know what is wrong with them.
SOCIAL WORKER: Is this something you'd like to talk about?

This question inquires whether this person would like to hire the worker for a service. Up until this time the worker is just stopping by to see how the client is doing. They have no previously set goals, and there is no understanding that the social worker is being used in a personal consultation framework.

In workshops people frequently ask us how one might engage clients in a desire-oriented conversation when the clients are not seeking consultation. Instead, consultants may be in a role where they do a home visit or bed visit or even a cell visit. Given our desire and customer orientation, the plausible concern about using this approach is: "If I am the one initiating the contact, I cannot start off the meeting by asking, 'What do you want in coming here?' "

However, just because we are initiating the contact does not mean that the person does not want something. In some situations, as the client begins to experience the consultant as an open and available person, s/he often decides to take advantage of the situation.

This concern is very salient. In order to set the context, we usually start off such meetings by explaining our role, how it is that we are there. If the context is medical social work, there would be an explanation of the worker's role. If the person is a crisis worker on a police call, that would be explained. If the person is a school counselor who is obliged by policy to see each student who has a failing grade, then that is explained. In these roles, we as consultants can ask how things are going and if there is anything the client would like to talk about. If it appears that the patient or client is concerned about something, we can then ask whether this is something s/he would like to talk about.

Now, back to the elderly woman and the social worker.

CLIENT: Well, it might do some good.

SOCIAL WORKER: So, this was quite disappointing to you that they did not come.

CLIENT: Yes, they had said that they might come on Sunday, but they called and said something about my grandson's having a hockey game and that they were sorry they did not have time to come by. I keep asking them to come by just for a little, but they don't care or something.

SOCIAL WORKER: Sounds like you really would like to have them stop by. How would it make a difference to you for them to come by more often?

As in the previous example, the client is talking about how she would like someone else to be different. The social worker is curious about how this change in someone else would make a difference to her, the client. This question introduces the idea that this desired change in someone else could be usefully thought of as a means to something else.

CLIENT: Well, I wouldn't feel so lonely and I'd feel like I'm a real person.

Of the two things she mentions, the social worker is more curious about the more positive one, "real person." The notion of feeling like or being respected as a "real person" has possibilities. Feeling like a real person can happen even if her loved ones do not visit as often.

SOCIAL WORKER: How do you mean—"a real person"?

CLIENT: Well, as if I mattered to someone. Like this morning, this girl comes here and gives me the same old cereal that I have told them over and over that I don't want. And there it was. I told her to take it back and dump it. (*angrily*)

SOCIAL WORKER: Guess you don't like the cereal, huh? Was that different for you to say so?

CLIENT: Yes, they treat you sometimes like you aren't here. So, I told her that even though I can't get out of bed, it doesn't mean that I should be treated that way.

SOCIAL WORKER: So, that is what you mean by being a real person.

While she may not get all of what she wants, that is, having her loved ones coming by and feeling that companionship, she may be able to do some things or recognize that she still matters. Sometimes, when people act as if they believe already that they are a real person, they find other ways to cope with being lonely. Sometimes, instead of complaining to loved ones, they are a bit more proactive. If they are acting that way, sometimes loved ones are likely to want to see them more than when they are complaining.

WANTING TO CHANGE ONE'S MOODS

Another example is a young man worried about his mood swings and his trust issues. He said that he had been in a long distance relationship for about a year now and that lately he found himself panicking when he knew his boyfriend was not home. He would wonder whether his boyfriend was out with someone else and what else he might be doing.

With all this he stated that he would like to be more trusting. He said that he would like to be more independent, like he imagined his sister and her boyfriend to be. He stated that his sister and her boyfriend both go off and do their own thing and do not think anything of being apart.

For him though of late, on a weekend when his partner did not fly in to Chicago to meet him or when he did not fly out to stay with his partner, there was a problem. On Friday nights especially, he would stay at home and worry about what his partner was up to and wait by the phone until late in the evening when his boyfriend would call.

We began to discuss possible signs to him that he was being more "trusting" in the way he wanted. He initially stated things in the negative. He would not be worried. He would not be pressing his boyfriend for details of where he was, whom he was with, and so on. Then, he said another sign, "My mind would not be focused on Friday night on what he might be doing. I would be saying, 'Good for him that he is doing things. I am glad he is out. I do not need to worry.'"

I asked if this was true. Did he really want his friend to go out? He said yes, that he wanted him to be happy and that he did not think it was healthy for him to make his boyfriend stay home.

We went on discussing for a while how he thought his partner was trustworthy. He maintained that his boyfriend had never given him any reason to be suspicious or paranoid. That is what bothered him so much about his own reaction of suspiciousness. It seemed unwarranted and it was such a waste of energy on his part.

I asked him further how he thought it *would make a difference to him* if he were more trusting and all this was resolved.

CLIENT: I would be enjoying the relationship to the fullest. Right now, I am either worrying about him or fighting with him over all my questions of him. I think he is getting more upset with me that I do not trust him.
CONSULTANT: So, you would be enjoying the relationship.
CLIENT: Yes, when we are together and not fighting about this we are very good. We have such fun.
CONSULTANT: That's more of what you want.
CLIENT: Yes, and Monday through Thursday, I wouldn't be thinking about Friday and I wouldn't be restricting myself. I'd be going out with a friend rather than getting into a bad mood about this.

CONSULTANT: Rather than getting into a mood, you would go do your own stuff.

CLIENT: I will be enjoying myself because I won't be restricting myself because of the mood. I will be saying the day is better because I have someone in my life. It will balance out again. (*Perhaps his shift from "would" to "will" indicates his increased confidence.*)

Introducing this notion of the significance of change into the inquiry inspires a conversation about what he wants beyond this immediate change in his "mood," of which he thinks he is a victim. The idea of being more trusting opens up for him the opportunity to talk about how he would be enjoying the relationship. My hope for him is that this discussion of his enjoying the relationship will allow him to talk in positive language of what will be happening. This discussion creates a story of what he ultimately wants, "enjoying the relationship."

This new storying allows him more options. If before he was thinking his only option was to bite his tongue and not bring up his suspicions as something he had to do in order to enjoy the relationship, he can now think the other way as well. By thinking about how much he enjoys the relationship, he can free himself to go out with a friend or seek more balance for himself rather than restrict himself by his mood.

A couple options have opened up here for him. One, he could contain his temptations to bring up his suspicions to his boyfriend by reassuring himself that confrontation was not helpful. Two, he could do something different. He could get into his own activities and demonstrate to himself and his lover that he could enjoy himself. What he found was that when he went to his health club or out with friends on Friday nights, he was not as concerned about his trust in his boyfriend and had other things to talk about when his boyfriend called.

WANTING TO CHANGE THINGS THAT ARE IMPOSSIBLE

This example is a telescoped version of an extended conversation.

ONCOLOGY COUNSELOR: So, how are things going today?

CLIENT: Well, you know I am going home soon.

COUNSELOR: Yes, I heard your treatments are just about finished.

CLIENT: I just wish I wasn't so sick.

COUNSELOR: How do you mean? How would it make a difference to not be sick?

CLIENT: I just wouldn't be so worried about my children.

She goes on to say how she cannot stop worrying about her small children and what is going to happen to them after she dies. She has a fatal cancer and very small children. She worries how her husband and her children will make it with her gone.

COUNSELOR: I am so sorry about all this. Is there some difference it would make for you to not have to worry?

CLIENT: If I wasn't so worried, I think I could begin to think about saying good-bye. (*She begins to cry.*)

COUNSELOR: This is what you would like—is to begin thinking about actually saying good-bye?

CLIENT: I need to start talking about it.

The conversation opens up as the storying moves beyond not being sick and not being so worried. As she mentions her desire to start talking about how the absence of those things would make a difference, she states that she would like to begin talking about dying and saying good-bye.

Each of the above examples shows how the conversation can open up as the consultant and client inquire about the possible differences or changes that could come about. The use of this construct, the significance of change, is merely a tool. We do not assume that there are some desires that are means and others that are ends. If we were to look at some examples of language, we would not be able to distinguish some concepts as definitely means and others as ends. If the above client had said that she wanted to no longer have a fatal disease, we would not think of the absence of a fatal disease as necessarily a means toward something else or as necessarily having some significance.

However, we can still introduce the construct and see what difference the construct makes on the conversation. In this example, the client said that one of the significances or consequences for her would be that she would no longer feel the need to worry about her children. No longer worrying about her children seems like a big step from no longer having a fatal disease. No longer worrying is beginning to sound more open to possibilities. We could inquire at that point if there were some other way that she would rather be thinking of her children. Since she would rather not be worrying, perhaps there is some other way that she would prefer to be thinking about them.

On the other hand, we could ask again what significance the absence of worrying would have. In this case, she said she could then begin to say good-bye. What she said up until that point sounded as if she thought that she could not or did not want to say good-bye as long as she was frightened of what might happen to her children when she was gone.

We do not think of her now talking about saying good-bye as a solution. Instead, we think of it as something else that she would prefer at this time and a further development within the conversation. Her preference about saying good-bye does not take away from her wanting to not have the cancer or her not wanting to worry. However, this preference appears to be something that she dearly wants even if the other two cannot be changed or accomplished.

Using the significance of change question in this instance does not mean that the absence of cancer or the absence of worry is a means to being able to say good-bye. However, choosing to think of them that way allows the conversation to extend into this other preference of saying good-bye.

Inquiry into the significance of change is thus not limited to only times when we think of the client's desire as a means to something else. This question can be used anytime and over and over. It is a tool for creating a more open conversation that can lead to further preferences or possibilities. The only criteria for when to explore the possible significance is when the conversation seems over-focused or confined, when the conversation seems to be going nowhere or in circles.

In the next chapter, we discuss how preferences can be expanded through the use of "sign" language.

CHAPTER SEVEN

Inquiring of Possibilities through "Sign" Language

From Linear Thinking to Brainstorming

In opening up the conversation for preferences and possibilities, we have found that the language of "signs" and possible "indications" facilitates an atmosphere that is open and creative.

It is our assumption that language can limit our experience or it can expand it. Working under another assumption—that more possibilities and options are better than fewer—we attempt to expand the language and storying that we are doing. Let us offer a perceptual metaphor for what we are talking about.

In our workshops we often ask participants to do an exercise that concretizes the experience of more possibilities. We ask everyone in the workshop to look around the room and identify at least five objects in the room that are the color *beige*. We further instruct them that when they have identified five objects they should each raise their hand. After everyone has had the opportunity to do this, we ask for a volunteer who could name the five beige objects s/he noticed.

As the volunteer is about to identify the five beige objects s/he has noticed, we interrupt and ask instead for the person to quickly tell us something in the room that s/he has noticed that is blue. Usually, with this quick interruptive instruction, the volunteer laughs at the irony of the situation. S/he cannot think of anything that is blue and so needs to search the room again for something blue.

When we laugh with participants and ask why they could not immediately come up with an object that was blue, they say, "I couldn't because I was looking for beige." We then ask, "So, what did you have to do to come up with a blue object?" They say, "I had to look again." "Were there no blue objects in the room the first time you looked around?" we ask. "Yes, there were, but I was not looking for them. I was looking for beige," they respond.

Everyone enjoys the exercise because it highlights so concretely our selective perception.

We explain that this is how we imagine our clients are experiencing their lives when they come in. We ask why they are coming to see us. They describe their situation as if everything were beige. They say, "My life is beige. I feel beige. I hate beige." As consultants we say, "I'm sorry things are so beige for you. Can you tell me what would be some signs that things were going more the way you want?" A client would possibly say, "Well, there might be some other colors in my life, a little red, a little green, or a little blue perhaps, maybe even a song in the air." With this new story of colors and a song, we suggest that, when the client goes home, s/he keep her eyes and ears open for any times when s/he notices some other colors or even a song.

This beige story gets at what we are about by inviting people to talk about what they *do* want and what would be some *signs* to them that what they want was actually happening. As the language opens up, clients can begin to create and identify other colors and signs as possibilities or alternatives to the beige.

As we mentioned in previous chapters, this reasoning is part of our desire to get out of the problem/solution distinction altogether. If one is thinking that either the problem or the solution is beige, one is trapped by the narrowness of the language. On the other hand, talking about what one wants and what might be some possible signs that it was happening opens up the language and conversation beyond the problem and solution altogether.

This exercise also highlights how this languaging, storying, and conversational approach differs from the assumptions of traditional goal-oriented approaches. In traditional goal-oriented approaches, client and therapist identify the goal for the therapy. They may also begin to talk about the goal in concrete, specific, and positive terms. At that point a different assumption enters the conversation. The therapist, thinking that the goal is a concrete target in the future or taking a visualization metaphor too literally, begins to shape the discussion toward what the client would *have to do* in order to accomplish the goal. This instrumental reasoning assumes that what the client wants is a concrete fact, that it is not happening now, and that it requires action on the client's part in order to make the goal happen.

For example, for the client who says that he wants to be less stressed and more relaxed with his work, instrumental goal-oriented questions would be:

- What do you have to do to accomplish that?
- What would be a first step?
- How are you going to do that?
- How ready are you to do that?
- How are you going to motivate yourself to do that?

- How are you going to get yourself to do that?
- What stops you now from doing that?
- If it's a fear that stops you, what do you need to get over that fear?

All of these questions presuppose that the client is not moving forward now, that he is stopped right now, and that some action needs to be taken.

Sign language opens up the conversation because it does not assume that the client is stopped or blocked or that some action has to be taken. With the same client, the conversation might go more like this:

CONSULTANT: What might be some *signs* to you that you were being more relaxed?

CLIENT: Well, I would be more *detached*.

CONSULTANT: (*"Detached" seems rather vague and I am curious about what it may mean more specifically.*) How do you mean? (*I could also ask, "What would be signs of detached?" or "Could you describe that more for me?"*)

CLIENT: I would not be worrying whether everyone is on the same page and doing their part. I think I wouldn't be trying to buttonhole everyone in the project and trying to get them in gear. I would *let it happen as it happens.*

CONSULTANT: You would let it happen? (*I am more curious about what positively would be happening than what might not be.*)

CLIENT: Yes, it is not all my responsibility. Others would take their responsibility or the project would just take a little longer.

CONSULTANT: So, you would let everybody have their responsibility. What would tell you that you were letting others have their responsibility?

The temptation in linear thinking is to ask, "What do you have to do to make that happen?" We assume that as the language changes within conversation, the client may notice things that he is already doing or he might choose to do something in the future. We do not assume that he necessarily has to do something in order to let others have the responsibility. Instead another *sign* question was asked.

CLIENT: I would *be enjoying those parts of the project that interest me* and *letting people in on what I am doing.*

CONSULTANT: How do you mean?

CLIENT: Now, I am so focused on what I have to do and what everyone else is not doing. I think I would notice what others are doing that is interesting and talking about what is going on in my research.

CONSULTANT: So, you would notice yourself talking with others about what they are doing and what you are doing. Anything else?

CLIENT: I would not be thinking about work when I am at home. *My girlfriend would notice that I was more relaxed.*

CONSULTANT: So, you would be leaving work at work and thinking of other things or doing other things when you are home?

CLIENT: Exactly, *at home I would be doing more of the things that I enjoy and that my girlfriend wants to do.*

CONSULTANT: How do you mean?

CLIENT: I would be *biking and cooking.* I want to work to live, not live to work.

CONSULTANT: So you would be doing things you like and living more?

CLIENT: Yes.

CONSULTANT: And your girlfriend would notice that you were more relaxed?

CLIENT: *Yes, she would say I was more patient, that rather than being in a rush to get out of a store, that I was calm and cool.*

This dialogue appears very artificial because of the shortening and the repetition of the same questions. Normally, there would be more discussion of each sign the client is bringing up. He has mentioned several things that he might notice.

He initially mentions his being more detached, not worrying about others, letting it happen, letting others be responsible or letting the project take longer, enjoying parts of the project, talking with others over their interests and his, relaxing when he was home rather than thinking about work, doing what he and his girlfriend want, and his girlfriend noticing his patience and calmness. I would ask him to expand and explain each of these signs to me.

All of the things he mentioned are like the "colors" of the previous exercise. These signs are not discussed as things that he now has to commit to doing. We are not going to ask him the traditional goal-achievement questions of linear or instrumental thinking. These are developments of the conversation opening up, and these are ways that he might recognize that things are going more the way he wants. There is no expectation that he has to go out and do any of these things. He may chose to do some of them or he may—through this new story of *detachment, letting it happen, letting others have responsibility, enjoying what he wants both in and out of work and working to live*—recognize how he is already doing some of these things. Frequently, in these conversations, clients spontaneously recognize how they already do some of these things.

Discussion of what clients want, the possible significance of their having what they want, and the signs of what they want opens up the language and the conversation. With this opening up, the client may recognize that many of the other "colors" from the beige story may already be happening. The client may recognize many more possibilities both already in her or his experience or potentially in the future.

Using sign language in this manner is intended just to generate possibilities of a client-preferred future. It is not intended as in early solution-focused brief therapy to generate how the client would know there was a solution (de Shazer, 1988).

For us, "sign languaging" is more metaphorical. It is like the mind-mapping articulated by Tony Buzan in *Using Both Sides of Your Brain* (1974). Buzan talks about mapping ideas in a nonlinear fashion. He states something that many of us writers recognize from experience. If in planning a writing project, a writer immediately tries to outline what s/he is going to write, the project seems to bog down. The bogging down seems to take place because of the constraints of having to think in linear terms of what should come first and then second. As a writer's attention gets focused on what should be the logical form or organization, the creative process gets lost.

Instead, he suggests that one merely write in the middle of the page what one wants to write about and then surround this topic with whatever associations one has. For example, one of the early mind-maps for this book is shown on page 96.

All of these ideas were associations that we had at the beginning to the initially stated goal of having a book about advances in brief therapy. If we had started in a linear fashion, asking ourselves, "What should we say first?" or "What is most important to say first, second, etc.?" we would probably still be thinking about it rather than your reading this page.

We borrowed the notion of signs initially from the discourse of first-order cybernetics and rocket guidance systems. In cybernetics and guidance systems, the notion of signs is used to distinguish information or indications that would be feedback that the rocket is on target. Rockets have radar systems that send out signals to various objects. The return signal is information to the computer. The information is matched against what should be the time of the signal's return. This comparison tells the computer whether the rocket is on course to the target. The indications are feedback to tell the rocket computer whether to remain on its present course or alter it. The information is also feedback to indicate when the rocket has reached its goal.

As we translated this language into a pragmatic-conversational understanding, we realized its creative and freeing potential, not as a metaphor for guidance and control, but for creating stories of possibilities. The notion of signs and the metaphor of mind-mapping seem to fit with the nonlinear complexities of human events and suggest spontaneous ways to influence them.

Inquiry in this direction can follow from questions like this:

*So, when things are going more the way you want, what might be some **signs** to you that things are going more the way you want?*

SIGNS OF WHAT THE CLIENT WANTS

Let us pick up the story from chapter five of the man who had initially been ordered to come to a counselor for marijuana use. He had stated in the first meeting that he wanted to keep his job. He stated in the second meeting that

he wanted to "keep his job and deal with it." This was his indication that he wanted something from coming to the consultation and his initiation into preferencing.

CONSULTANT: So, what might be some signs to you that you were dealing with it and keeping your job?
CLIENT: Well, I guess I wouldn't be thinking about it. There wouldn't be this tension and stress.
CONSULTANT: You would be thinking about other things?

He states what would not be happening. I invite him to consider what would be happening that would tell him that he was "keeping his job and dealing with it."

CLIENT: I suppose *I would be thinking about what else I want to do with my time.*
CONSULTANT: How do you mean?
CLIENT: Well, if I wasn't smoking, I guess I would want to do something else, not just hanging out with the TV. *Maybe my wife and I would do more together.*
CONSULTANT: Really, you would like to do that?
CLIENT: Yeah. Right now I smoke because I just want to get away from things, just be by myself and away from everything—not worrying. I suppose I would like to be relaxed and enjoying time with my wife and my kid.
CONSULTANT: You don't want to be worrying. You want to be enjoying time with your family. Tell me more about that. What would be signs that you were relaxing either with them or alone?

I merely ask him to expand on this story creation by asking what would be possible signs of "enjoying time with your family."

CLIENT: I guess I would just be doing things with my kid. I know the worrying doesn't do anything anyway.
CONSULTANT: No, what makes you say that?
CLIENT: Cause, it hardly makes any difference. It just puts me in a bad mood.
CONSULTANT: So, you would be putting the worrying aside and spending time with your kid and your wife. How else would it make a difference to put the worries aside or do something else?
CLIENT: I think that maybe I wouldn't be so serious. Maybe I would enjoy things a little more.
CONSULTANT: Hmm. What would tell you that you were enjoying things a little more?
CLIENT: Maybe, I would just say, *"What the hell?"* and go do it.
CONSULTANT: Sounds better for you. But, aren't there things that maybe you should be worrying about or taking seriously?

Many times clients state what they want as the total elimination of some activity like worrying. At the same time, what happens is that the more they attempt to put the worrying out of their mind, the more worried they become. So, I am curious if there are not some things he would like to think about or if there is not some other way he could deal with these concerns in a productive way.

CLIENT: Not really. I know that I got most things covered. *I just need to let go a little.*

He says no. Instead, he seems to indicate that he thinks he has most of these concerns taken care of. He seems to recognize already that maybe it would be okay to just let go a little.

In this interchange, the client says several things both negative and positive that would let him know that he was "dealing with it." The language actually extends beyond "dealing with it" as he talks about wanting to "relax and spend more time with his wife and child." The conversation then extends into not taking things so seriously and his letting go.

To someone who is not familiar with sign questions or significance questions, this interchange might sound like a broken record. Clients have generally reported, however, that they were not aware that we repeated the same questions. They were most aware of the consultant's interest and their talking more about what they wanted.

SIGNS OF FURTHER CHANGE

Another example is a man who came in and began talking about his having been suspended by his employer for missing several days of work. He had been drinking so heavily that he was very sick and missed work without calling. He voluntarily decided to do something and made the call to his insurance company for a referral.

As he was describing his situation, he mentioned that he had not had a drink in several days. I asked how he was doing this to see both if this was different on his part and how this not drinking might fit with what he wanted from coming to see me.

He said this was different and that he was feeling a little better. He said he was trying AA and mostly he was trying self-restraint. When I asked how he was managing the restraint, he said "knowing his situation" was the biggest help. He felt that if he did not do something now, he would never stop drinking.

It is very common for people who come to a first consultation to report some difference or change. We ask and invite the clients to expand more on the possible stories of difference and success. More on this will follow in the next chapter.

At this time in the meeting, since we had already been discussing some successes, the sign language that seemed to fit was:

*What would be **further** signs that things were going the way you want?* or *What would be signs that things were going **even more** the way you want?*

CONSULTANT: So, you have begun to make some changes, restraining yourself, knowing the seriousness of your situation, and going to AA. What would be signs that things were going even more the way you want?

CLIENT: I wouldn't have the urge to drink or something like that. Some of these crazy thoughts I have wouldn't be there.

Clients often cite what *wouldn't* be happening as a sign. The absence of drinking or the urge to drink can be a helpful hindsight. In other words, clients' recognizing that they have gone a day without a drink can build confidence. It can be a marker that progress is being made, but it does not give them things to notice in the present as they are going through the day and into their future. Noticing things not happening is certainly part of the story, but at some time we want to invite the creation of positive signs of what they *will* notice.

CONSULTANT: There would be other thoughts you would rather have or just that these thoughts wouldn't be there?

CLIENT: I used to be involved in sports pretty much and things like that. I'm older now but it seems like I've given up a lot of my interests. It would be nice to wake up and, instead of having a drink, maybe I'd *go bowling that day or play softball, or work out at the gym.*

CONSULTANT: So, you're thinking of getting back to those kinds of interests?

CLIENT: Yeah, instead of sitting at a bar.

CONSULTANT: So, you'd be developing other interests.

CLIENT: Yes, I never used to be a *big reader but I used to be involved in mysteries and so on.*

CONSULTANT: So, you would be doing other things.

CLIENT: If I could afford it, I would like to *travel again.* I traveled when I was in the service. Of course that wasn't fun travel. That was mostly on military transports. But I got to see places.

CONSULTANT: You like traveling?

CLIENT: My girlfriend and I have talked about going up to Michigan. Her uncle has some cottage or farmhouse up there. But I've been the one to hold things back. I hid behind a bottle. I would just like to be doing things normal people do instead of hiding behind a bottle.

CONSULTANT: So, you want to go even up there? What makes you want to do that?

Asking clients to explain their desire can be an invitation for them to expand on it and story even more their *thinking of, wanting to,* and *deciding to* do something for themselves.

CLIENT: It is nice to get out of the city, get some different air, get out where it is more open.

CONSULTANT: This is something your girlfriend would like to do as well?

CLIENT: Yes, she used to go up a lot to her uncle's even as a child. She always asked me but I said no. Or she was afraid to ask because she was afraid I'd have a few on Friday night and be too hungover to drive on Saturday. She can drive but she was afraid of my driving.

CONSULTANT: And what might be different is that she would ask you and you might say, "Yes."

CLIENT: Possibly.

CONSULTANT: Or you might suggest it?

CLIENT: There might be even more *ideas that come out of this head as it clears, not have my thoughts so narrow. Expand my horizons a little.*

The conversation has now shifted away from just the lack of drinking being a sign to talking about what else he might want to be doing or thinking about. He is now talking about "expanding my horizons a little."

CONSULTANT: What else might be a sign?

I asked, "What else might be a sign?" However, I was also curious about "expanding my horizons" and could have asked what he meant by that or what would be signs to him that he was "expanding his horizons."

CLIENT: That's kind of tough. I never was really close to my family, but *maybe I'd see them more.*

CONSULTANT: Would that be good or more of a temptation?

CLIENT: It would be good. Only my grandmother has a problem with alcohol. I've been avoiding them.

CONSULTANT: Anybody else who knows about your change besides your girlfriend and boss?

CLIENT: I told my mother so she wouldn't worry.

CONSULTANT: How did you decide to tell her?

CLIENT: I've always been an introvert. Maybe it would be good to tell other people what's going on with me.

The conversation has now evolved to his talking about how he would like to be spending more time with his family rather than avoiding them and involving himself exclusively with alcohol. He now is developing several possible ways that he may recognize that he is making progress and getting what he wants. Whereas before he may have had only one way to recognize change, that is, the absence of drinking, now he has several. He might be back into or developing other interests, doing sports, reading, traveling, maybe accepting his girlfriend's invitation, spending more time with his family, and telling more people what is going on with him.

In the remainder of this meeting he talked about how difficult it would be to tell his drinking friends that he was not drinking now. He said that he was actually afraid to talk to them for fear that they would try to talk him into coming down to the bar. For now, he thought it best to not talk to them, but eventually he thought it would be good to tell them he was not drinking so that they would not call.

The remaining meetings with him followed his pace, which was slow and careful. He continued to explain his making his change because of his fear of what would happen to him. He turned down his girlfriend's invitation to go out to dinner because of his fear of exposure to drinking at the restaurant. He also told her he could not attend a wedding with her because of the same fear. She was very angry with him for saying no at the last minute, but he decided it was better to be cautious.

When he eventually did go out on a dinner date with her, he was very proud how he managed to enjoy the time out and enjoy the food. Before, he never paid too much attention to the food.

This storying of signs went cautiously as we followed his pace. In each succeeding meeting we talked about his successes since the last time and we also talked about what would be further signs of his continued progress.

SIGNS AFTER SETBACKS

Sign language can be very useful when clients come in and talk about bad times or setbacks. Asking them what will be signs to them that they are getting back on track can normalize the idea of setbacks as opposed to failures. Sign talk can also create possibilities of recognizing overall progress even with setbacks. A sample question might go like this:

*What might be some **signs** that you were getting back on track?*

A man came in for his second meeting with me. In the first meeting he said that he needed to stop bingeing with cocaine. He said he had been to NA before and had even gone through an inpatient treatment program. However, he thought that he had only been dancing with sobriety. He was never convinced he needed to stop and he thought that maybe he would quit for a while. He said that he needed to stop because it was costing him his marriage. His wife had thrown his clothes out of the house. He said he needed to be active in sobriety again. Beyond that he thought he needed to handle his anger differently. He would react to his wife's confrontations with angry fits, in which he had broken things in the house. One time he had damaged his car when he left the house after an argument with her. He did not want to do this with her and he could not stand the guilt afterward.

At the end of that meeting, I reflected that it sounded like he was recognizing what his continued use was going to cost and that I wanted to encourage him to continue the efforts and steps he had made the past several days. He had found an NA meeting and had been going. He was looking for a sponsor, and he was looking to be honest with himself. I suggested that he do two things: (1) notice what happens at those times when he thinks of coke and does something else* and (2) notice those times when he was handling other parts of his life the way he wanted to. This was in reference to his statement that he wanted both to be honest with himself and to be himself. He did not feel that he was being himself when he acted out of anger and resentment toward his wife or when he acted out of guilt and tried to make up for what he had done.

When he returned the second time, I asked what was different since the last meeting. He said that two days before our meeting he had gone on a coke binge. He mentioned that the previous Sunday he had gone over to see his coke buddy in the afternoon. They smoked until they ran out. However, he left early that evening. I was curious if that was different. I was wondering if in the past he would have stayed much longer. He said that it was different. Normally, his binges lasted at least 24 hours. However, he did not see this as an occasion of his taking some initiative to shorten his binge or as a sign of his choosing to do something different with regard to coke. He described this as an occasion of his being revolted by what he had done and by his friend who was totally losing control. His friend was not eating, he had no money, and he seemed very paranoid.

I thought of his revulsion as different and as perhaps part of his deciding to be active in sobriety again. However, his having binged on coke seemed to loom larger to him than any shortening of the binge or anything else that might indicate some progress on his part. So, since he was describing this binge as a slip, I assumed that he wanted to get back to active sobriety.

CONSULTANT: So, it sounds like you want to get back to being active with your sobriety. Is that right?

CLIENT: Yes, I will be going to a meeting right after I leave here tonight.

CONSULTANT: So, *what will tell you* that your slip is over and that you are on track with your active sobriety again?

CLIENT: One thing is that *I will be acknowledging what I did*. When I see my wife I'll be telling her. I won't be trying to explain it away and I won't be arguing with her.

CONSULTANT: How would this make a difference to her or to you?

CLIENT: It won't make that much difference to her. She will just go postal again. She will call me a bum and all that crap. But I will know it is different. I will know that I am being honest with myself.

CONSULTANT: How do you mean?

CLIENT: If this happened before, I would be arguing with her because of her trying to hang me with it. But what's important here is not that she is right. I know she is right, I messed up and it is up to me to do right.

CONSULTANT: So, before you couldn't stand this lording over you?

---

*This suggestion is taken from de Shazer and Molnar (1984).

CLIENT: Yeah, but in a way I cannot be thinking of her.
CONSULTANT: Uh-huh. What else would be a *sign* that you were back to active sobriety?
CLIENT: If I was *taking things slower.*
CONSULTANT: How would that be a sign?
CLIENT: Cause, being stressed out is my cop-out for bingeing. I get all worked up trying to make up for what I have done or I try to make everything right. So, it's not enough that I apologize—I gotta be superdad. I promise I will do everything for everybody.
CONSULTANT: So, as you are taking things slower, you won't be a superdad, you will be . . .
CLIENT: I'll just do a regular day. This "one day at a time" is finally making sense. If I slip, the idea is not to make up for it, I just do right the next day.

In this example, the client has had a slip and appears very disappointed and angry with himself. The conversation does not seem open to storying this past week as any kind of success (more about storying success will be discussed in the next chapter). The client and I could go back to what he was initially talking about in the first meeting, that is, talking more about his preferences. On the other hand, since he already mentioned his desire to be active in sobriety, we could talk about what would be further signs to him of his being active in his sobriety or his getting back "on track" with his sobriety. That was the preference I chose.

SIGNS OF PROGRESS

Sometimes, clients initially talk about what is stopping them from making desired change or about what they want in the distant future. Rather than trying to explore or deconstruct what they think is blocking them, we invite them to consider what would be signs that they were making progress and were not stopped. While they might be thinking in black-and-white terms, either blocked or not blocked, the notion of progress introduces the idea of process. Within process the client can still be troubled and yet have a sense of movement.

A sample question would be simply:

*What would be some **signs** that you were making progress?*

An example is a man who thinks he is stuck in his research project. We do not discuss what will be the signs to him that his project is finished. Instead, he is saying that, rather than being stuck, he wants to be working or moving forward. This example also shows the interweaving of the use of sign language and the discussion of successes. Discussion of successes is something we will discuss in more detail in the next chapter.

In response to the opening question of what he wants from coming to see me, he tells me about his concern. He states that his sense is that he is stuck and making no progress. He also states how much he has reflected on this whole process and that he thinks that, in part, his concerns about other things have turned into excuses not to work. Instead of working he begins to worry about how people might criticize his project, about what he is going to do once he graduates from school, and, on the other hand, what will happen if he does not get this work done.

In summarizing his situation, he says, "I'm stuck and these upset feelings just distract me or I let them keep me from getting things done."

CONSULTANT: So, tell me, then, what would be *signs* that the situation had changed and that you were making the progress you want?

CLIENT: I would be *using my time better,* meaning I would be using most of my available time to work. That would mean that of the time that I have now where I am not obliged to do other things, *I would be using seventy-five percent of that time.*

Like today, I am usually free most of the day. Instead of working at nine o'clock, I don't go to school until noon. Then I have a cup of coffee and then I obsess about what I am going to teach in my night class. Before I know it, almost all the afternoon is gone. That's not true. I do know what I am doing. I am distracting myself from what I should be doing. Sometimes I read a little and tell myself that the reading will be helpful when I do my analysis later. But I know what I am doing, I am just distracting myself from what I want to do.

The thing is that I have been aware of this for a long time, but the awareness of this and how I feel is not getting me to do anything about it.

CONSULTANT: So, instead of this, what would be *signs* that things were going differently?

CLIENT: The signs would be that I would be *sitting at the computer, entering data, finishing up the last piece of the questionnaire, and coding the vignette.* If I actually sat down, the coding would take no more than a few hours. But I cannot get myself to do it.

He mentions this initial behavioral description of possible signs as if the actual work would be easy. I am confused by his saying that it would be such an easy matter and his also saying that he cannot do it. So, I ask him what makes him think this is possible.

CONSULTANT : What makes you think it would be such a snap?

CLIENT: Because I have done this before. I know it can go that quickly. I just stopped.

CONSULTANT: When you did that before, were there not temptations to obsess about?

CLIENT: Yes, I just did it.

He has brought up how the work is possible because he has done it before. I am intrigued by how he managed to do it before even when he was tempted to be distracted.

CONSULTANT: How do you mean? It sounds like it is not very interesting stuff.

CLIENT: No, it is quite boring. I don't know how I did it. I did not pay attention at the time.

CONSULTANT: So, did someone twist your arm or how did you do it?

CLIENT: No, there was a period when it was exciting and I think I just ran down. I got sick and then I had to help my parents move. So, I just got out of the routine.

CONSULTANT: So, one of the signs would be *this routine.* What else?

CLIENT: I would be *getting to school by 9:00 and by 10:15 I'd be at the computer entering data.*

CONSULTANT: Now, my guess is that there would still be opportunities for temptations or distractions. What would be signs to you that you were making progress even if there were temptations or you got distracted for a bit?

Oftentimes, clients describe their goals in black-and-white terms. He states his situation as if he would be working all the time with no distractions or worries. I am curious about another possibility, that he could be distracted or worried and still making progress.

Client: I would be *reminding myself that if I don't get the boring part over, I'll never get to the exciting part.*

A little later in the meeting the client mentioned another worry.

CLIENT: One of the things that gets in the way is my worry of what I am going to do once this research is done. I have no plans and no full-time job in the works.

CONSULTANT: So, this is a worry. When your sense is that you are making progress, are you thinking that somehow this will no longer be a concern?

CLIENT: Well no. I mean I cannot really do anything about a job now. *So, I guess I will just be putting that aside and reminding myself of what is going on now.*

The storying here seems to be of making progress where he will notice himself doing some of things he wants to on his project, putting aside his worries until the work is done, and reassuring himself that, even if the work seems boring, it will be exciting again.

Several weeks later, the client reflected that in this meeting he recognized that he had gotten out of his routine. All he had to do was get into the routine again and the other worries about the future would take care of themselves. This apparently was doable, where the attempts at insight had been self-defeating. The inquiry into signs of progress allowed him to brainstorm or free associate to possibilities of progress without the worries as well as with the worries.

Sign language can be used in many ways. It can be used to talk about signs of clients' getting what they want, signs of their getting back on track, signs that they are making progress, signs of their recovering from a slip, or signs of further progress.

SIGNS WITH MORE THAN ONE PERSON

The inviting of sign language is also useful in meeting with a couple or family or anytime when you are meeting with more than one person. As one person talks about what would be signs to her/him of her/his preferences or describes what would be signs that the relationship was going more to her/his liking, the spouse or other person gets to listen in on what this desired relationship would look like.

In some relationships, this describing in positive terms can be very different if the partners' previous conversations or arguments were focused mostly on what would *not* be happening.

CONSULTANT: What are you wanting from coming here?
HUSBAND: The main thing is communication. We can't seem to talk about some of our problems or come to some consensus or solutions.
CONSULTANT: So, you are looking for ways to talk about things.
HUSBAND: I think that would help.

I turn to her now to begin with her as well. She begins by saying that coming here was her idea. Things for her have been upsetting for quite some time. However, only after seeing another counselor individually did she feel it was important enough to seek marriage counseling about her concerns.

Wife: Part of what is upsetting me about all this is that I don't feel connected with him anymore, no intimacy. I don't feel we connect very well. I don't know. I saw this problem starting a long time ago but I didn't want to deal with it. I'm hoping to change that because I cannot stand it anymore.

She explains more of how she sees connection as important to her now because they are both struggling with parenting two young children. I invite them to discuss what would be signs that their relationship was going more the way they would want. His preferences were initially "communication" and coming to "consensus or solutions." Her language initially was around "connection."

I am hoping to give them the opportunity to describe or create possible signs for themselves and the other.

CONSULTANT: So what would be some *signs* that your relationship was going more the way you want?

WIFE: We wouldn't be jumping to conclusions about what the other one was saying or what was behind what they were saying. *The communication would be clear and there wouldn't be any polluted messages.*

Of the possibilities of inquiry at this point I am most curious about the positive thing she states, which is that the communication would be "clear." As I ask about this, he begins to talk of what would be signs to him of "clear" and I summarize.

CONSULTANT: *She'd be responding to the words you said rather than assuming and if she were unhappy or unsure, she would say so.*

HUSBAND: *We'd be responding to what's concrete.*

CONSULTANT: How would that make a difference?

I am wondering how this focus on the concrete would make a difference to him and how he thinks it may make a difference to her. It seems to me that concreteness may be one of the things they argue about. In other words, perhaps he argues for her to be more concrete and she says, "Yes, but you are missing what I want to say." So, I think maybe the conversation might open up if we talk about how this concrete communication might make a difference. What is he hoping this concreteness may lead to that is not happening? Perhaps, this may open up what he is ultimately looking for and they can both talk about that instead of the means of getting there.

HUSBAND: Part of it is that I try to be thoughtful and sometimes I don't respond quickly enough for her. So, if she were responding to the words and understanding, I would have more time to assimilate what's happening.

CONSULTANT: So, her understanding would give you more time to reflect and try to assimilate. You want to reflect and assimilate what she says so that you can understand and she can feel understood.

HUSBAND: Exactly. I wish I could communicate more clearly that I am not trying to hide anything.

This could have been an opportune time to ask him what she would she say would be signs to her that he was attempting to understand. It may be that the only option he thinks he has at that time is to attempt to slow her down and be more concrete. This he would do in order for *him* to understand, but it might not help in terms of her feeling understood. It could be helpful for him to have that possibility as well. However, at the time I was curious about what might be further signs to him.

CONSULTANT: (*to husband*) And what would be *signs* to you?

HUSBAND: She can be critical. I find it hard to be with her that way. An example, she's in the kitchen and she asks for help. I come in and survey the situation. I start doing something that seems to need doing and she says, "That's not helpful." When I ask what she wants me to do, she says, "Isn't it obvious?" I feel trapped, no matter what I do.

CONSULTANT: Hmm. So, *what might tell you* it was going better?

HUSBAND: *If she said, "Can you do this?" or "Thank you."*

This positive description of signs that the situation was going better can be helpful for him and her. If there are occasions when she already does this, these occasions may stand out even more. If she is not doing this now, which is unlikely, she may have another possibility in terms of what she could do that might make a difference.

A little further on in the meeting, I again asked a sign question.

CONSULTANT: What would be other *signs* to you?

WIFE: If we *spent more time together*. We'd be together more. Seems like we are in different places. We are in the same house but not together. We'd be more *partners, more like us two*.

We spend our time apart. After the kids are in bed, we do separate things, time on the computer, dishes, those sorts of things.

CONSULTANT: So, what would be *signs* that things were going the way you want?

WIFE: We might be *talking together about plans*. We cannot do it at the dinner table. The kids are talking about school or their things.

CONSULTANT: They do want their attention, don't they.

WIFE: There would be a *plan for action*. A lot of time we talk about what I am unhappy about but we don't do anything about it.

CONSULTANT: So, part of the talking would be about *what you are going to do.*

WIFE: Yes, what he is going to do and what I am going to do. And we could express our differences.

A little later in the meeting, she talks about additional signs.

WIFE: *He'd be coming halfway.* I feel I come part way, but he doesn't.

CONSULTANT: So, he'd be trying on your idea?

WIFE: Hmm-hmm. He would be acknowledging how I feel. Now, he just says, "This is what we are going to do."

CONSULTANT: So, he would be . . .

WIFE: He would say, "*I can see that you're upset." Sometimes, I don't think he wants to hear my upset. Sometimes, I think he just writes off what I say and that he does not respect my opinion. I want him to say, "I'm trying to understand that you are upset."*

For example, we have different ideas about the children and what is safe. So, rather than dismissing my worries, he would at least acknowledge that some things bother me and respect that.

CONSULTANT: So, he would be listening to your worries, trying to understand, and let you know that he is trying to appreciate how you might feel that way. And, how would this make a difference for you or between you?

It seems that maybe she argues in order to be heard, not necessarily to fight about what she wants. She appears to want him to make some changes so that she can be heard. Perhaps it has been helpful for him to hear concretely what she wants, but I am also curious how the present conversation might open up even more if we discussed how this change in him might make a difference to her. Depending on what she says, this change that she is hoping for from him might take on a different significance.

WIFE: I think I might be willing to talk less emotionally. I probably would not get so worked up if he heard me and *I might make more of an effort to be calm.*

At the end of this meeting, I asked what we had talked about that was different or helpful. He said it was helpful to hear that she wanted to spend time together and to feel understood.

Frequently, at the end of a meeting like this, we suggest that when the partners go home they keep their eyes and ears open for any times when things go more the way they want. Frequently, what happens is that clients go home and choose to do something different based on what was discussed in the meeting. On the other hand, they are more sensitive to the signs and therefore notice what may already be occurring. They may notice what was already occurring because it is now drawn to their attention or it may have taken on a different significance.

For example, it may be new for him to hear that it is more important to her to feel understood by him than for him to agree. He may also be more sensitive to and more noticing of the times when she says "Thank you" or "Can you . . . ?" Another possibility is that it is new to hear that she wants to spend more time with him and do some planning.

For her, it may be new to hear that his response pace is slower than what she expects, because he is attempting to understand what she is saying and needs more time to do that.

In this chapter we have discussed the advantages and pragmatics of conversing with clients in a spontaneous or mind-mapping style as opposed to a linear or instrumental style. This inquiry of the future in terms of signs can introduce many possibilities. With these preferences and possibilities, clients can return to their everyday life with a different story, with a different way of thinking, with different perceptual lenses, or with different options for action.

With this new language of preferences and possibilities, clients often spontaneously mention times when these events are already occurring. In the next chapter, we discuss how we can story these preferences, differences, and possibilities that are already occurring in the present.

CHAPTER EIGHT

Inquiring of Differences and Successes

From Obstacles to Optimism

Inquiring of difference or success happens at no particular time in a predetermined sequence of consultation. It can happen at the beginning of the first meeting. Oftentimes, clients come in and spontaneously mention that recently things have been better. They may say that when they decided to call about getting help, they also decided to do some things differently, which made some things better. Other times conversation of difference or successes flows from discussion of what they want or from talking about what would be signs of their preferences. Conversation of success or change also takes place in succeeding sessions.

We are very intrigued by these conversations of difference and success. We express our intrigue, surprise, and excitement with our voice tone and by asking questions. We are curious about how the clients brought about these changes. We are curious even when they do not initially recognize themselves as having had any positive influence upon the situation.

This storying of success and empowerment can be facilitated with inquiries such as:

How did you do that?
How did you decide to do that?
How did you manage to do that?

As you take a careful look at these questions you will see that they are inquiring about, or asking the client to inquire about, their own possible influence upon the situation. "How did you do that?" assumes that the *client did* something. It assumes self-action, self-competence, and self-responsibility. Clients are invited through this question to create with the consultant a story of success in which they are the active, if not proactive, characters.

The second question, "How did you decide to do that?" presupposes an active decision on the client's part. Here we are inviting the client to create a story of making a conscious, deliberate choice.

In some ways we are asking clients to revise their story of their past or create a new story that may have empowering influences upon their future.

The reason for our using both terms, *difference and success*, is that sometimes clients do not recognize recent events as successful. They may say that recently everything has been the same or equally bad. By exploring whether an event was different, clients may begin to recognize some differences. By exploring how the difference led to different results, we and the clients may revise the story of what happened as not only different but also successful.

For example, couples often report that they are looking for fewer fights and better ways to communicate with each other. They report that the difficulty is not a problem with being close or intimate. They just get into fights over little things that escalate into shouting matches and extremely hurt feelings. Many of these couples do not see the ending of the fights as significant nor as having any potential for better communication.

However, by asking if it was different for a recent fight to not go longer, we sometimes find that couples will say yes. They report that other fights would go on for several hours or that the fight would continue the next day. The introduction of the notion of difference invites a different conversation and story creation. We are now talking about a short fight as opposed to a long one. We often ask how they decided to stop it sooner. They sometimes say something like each of them just realized that they did not want to fight anymore. If we ask if that was different for them to think that way, often they will say yes to that as well and explain that each of them realized the fight was not going to get them anywhere. They did not want to hurt each other. By the end of the conversation, they see the fight as different not only in being shorter but also from the point of view of how their thinking has changed. Stopping the fight could be described as a choice to do something different. This choice to stop the hurting and to do something different they now see as a success.

Here are some examples of how the disposition of curiosity can facilitate an open inquiry of difference or success and how these questions can facilitate stories that are self-empowering.

AT THE BEGINNING OF A FIRST MEETING

A client who came to see me spoke of her concerns at her place of employment. She said that recently a colleague had said that she did not know how to handle the client or what to do around her. The colleague said that the client's emotionalism—her getting upset and crying—confused her. She was afraid to talk to her for fear of upsetting her. The colleague was wondering what was wrong.

When I asked the client what she wanted from coming to see me, she said that she wanted to be "more in control of her emotions and to handle things." As she said this, she mentioned that in the past couple days she had been better. So, I inquired about it.

CLIENT: The last couple days I have been better.

CONSULTANT: How do you mean?

CLIENT: Ever since this other worker said this to me, I have been totally embarrassed. I knew that I was emotional and that I have been crying a lot, but to have someone else notice it and say something about it—I was shocked that she said this and totally embarrassed.

CONSULTANT: Seems like it makes it more embarrassing to have it be so public. So how do you mean that you have been better?

CLIENT: Well, one of our salesmen came in the other day and just went off on me. He started yelling in front of everybody else and telling me how I should not have assumed that he had not filled the order yet and telling that to his client. I did not break down.

CONSULTANT: You didn't? How did you do that?

I know that she said that she was better, but I am still surprised and happy for her that she managed to do that in what sounds like a very hurtful and upsetting situation.

CLIENT: Everybody knows this guy is a prima donna and an asshole. I was not going to give him the satisfaction of crying or breaking down. He was right but I was not going to let him keep on going. So, I just said I would take care of it and walked away.

CONSULTANT: How did you decide to do that?

CLIENT: I just knew that I did not want to break down in front of this guy and I knew that I could not break down in the office again.

CONSULTANT: So what did you do?

CLIENT: I walked away and went into the washroom. I got myself together. I mean he got me so mad and I felt hurt. I have done so much for this man. I have worked overtime to get out his orders. I have dropped other things because he has said his order is a rush. And then for him to say this in front of everybody else!

CONSULTANT: So, what did you do then?

CLIENT: I pulled together what I wanted to say and then I went to my supervisor and told her.

CONSULTANT: This was different for you to organize what you wanted to say?

Asking whether this was different can mark this story as different from what she had been doing that was problematic. She now has a story in hand of her doing something different and its being more successful.

CLIENT: I knew that if I didn't think about it first, I would make a fool of myself.

CONSULTANT: So, you thought about it first in terms of what you wanted to say and then went and talked to your supervisor. So, you and your supervisor ended up talking about him and not you.

CLIENT: Right.

CONSULTANT: And that is more of how you would like to be handling these kinds of situations?

CLIENT: Yes.

SUCCESS STORIES FLOWING FROM PREFERENCES

In chapter five, while we were talking about listening for and highlighting what clients say they want, we shared the dialogue with the young woman who talked of wanting to be more "responsible for what she does good and what she does bad." Let's rejoin that conversation to show how conversations can flow from talking about preferences to storying some recent success.

We left off with the client saying:

CLIENT: I would like to be taking responsibility for what I do good and what I do bad. Not sitting there placing blame on one thing or another. I think in that aspect I would get rid of a lot of anger.

You know I love my new job. It's going really well. I feel really good about it. In the same aspect, I notice that at jobs when I spend time with people from work outside of work as friends, my work deteriorates a little because I let work and personal time intertwine. I don't break between personal feelings and work. It all becomes one and then I take it personally.

CONSULTANT: So, you have noticed that does not work. So, tell me more about your wanting to take more responsibility for the good and the bad.

CLIENT: Well, driving down to the interview, my mother's telling me what to say and what to wear. I am really excited.

CONSULTANT: This is what you are saying?

CLIENT: No, this is what my mother is saying. I decided not to tell my dad. He would have just brought me down. So, I just thought this would be really great to get this job. The interview went really well. On the way home though I am saying, "I can't believe I did this. I don't deserve this. I'll just go back to waitressing at the pancake place. I am never going to get anywhere. I can't do this."

Given how she had just described her always taking good things and turning them into bad, I am curious how she managed this good thing.

CONSULTANT: How did you get yourself to interview at all?

CLIENT: I had no choice. I was so much in debt and with my income I could not even pay my bills. I have no money. I would normally just hit up my dad, listen to him bitch for a while, but in the end he would give me the money. But I did not like that begging or having to put up with his crap.

CONSULTANT: So, how did you decide to get another job?

CLIENT: I had no other choice.

CONSULTANT: But you could have gone to your dad again?

CLIENT: I know . . . I just felt like I didn't want to.

CONSULTANT: And you could have screwed up the interview.

CLIENT: I don't know. I guess I talked to myself and I played this game with myself. I know the person I want to be but I never would be it except in my own little world. I decided, "You know what! It is time I let this person out." And for some reason I felt phony in the interview, like I was someone made up.

So, I thought I'm going to play a part, a character of me.

CONSULTANT: Of what you want to be?

CLIENT: Yes.

CONSULTANT: And did it work?

CLIENT: I got the job!

And when I came back from DC from the fiasco with my dad, I got on the plane. First off, I got the cab in DC, paid the extra money to change my ticket, took a cab to my new place here in the city. I realized then, "You know what? I am capable of taking care of myself. My dad is not going to believe this that I did this on my own."

CONSULTANT: This was different for you?

CLIENT: I never stood up for myself and walked away. I thought to myself that I was not going to go out with my dad to hear him tell me how shitty I was. So, I just left DC and took my chances on getting home.

CONSULTANT: This was different?

CLIENT: Yeah, it was almost empowering . . .

CONSULTANT: Good for you! How'd you do that?

CLIENT: This is just something I needed to do. I feel like I don't need to play this other person anymore. I can *be* this person.

We are creating this story of the present in which she is doing things more the way she wants to. She is taking responsibility for her finances, going to and completing a successful interview, and experimenting with a different view of herself. The story expands as I invite her beyond her initial explanation that she went for the interview because, as she believes, she had no choice. She expands by talking about how she has this "other self" that she decided to play act.

Throughout this conversation, I am curious about what was different about what she did and how she did it.

SUCCESS STORIES FLOWING FROM
CONVERSATION OF SIGNS

Sometimes inquiring of success emerges from discussion of the signs of the preference. For example, a woman was describing signs that she was beyond problem drinking and that her life was going more the way she wanted. She had recently had her husband leave their apartment. She felt he was being abusive to her and taking advantage of her. She said she wanted to stop drinking and had recently been making efforts to stop. I asked what would be signs to her that her life was going more the way she wanted.

CLIENT: There would be some peace in my life, happiness. Some happiness.

CONSULTANT: So, there would be some happiness. And as you were experiencing that, what else would tell you things were more the way you want?

CLIENT: My kids would be coming around more.

CONSULTANT: How do you mean?

CLIENT: If I wasn't drinking, they would come around.

CONSULTANT: So, you are more convinced of that and would like them to come around. What else would tell you that things were better?

CLIENT: I would have some friends. Right now, I don't have any. And maybe I would be busy . . . go to the health club or the woman's group at church where I could be with people more.

CONSULTANT: So, you would have some things planned. Sounds like you know a little bit of what you would like to get back to.

CLIENT: Well, I have been wondering this to myself. I say to myself, "Wait a minute, I've had the courage to raise five children by myself and now I am thinking that I cannot take care of myself. Why? What happened?" This is what I am wondering.

CONSULTANT: Oh! That is something. So, it sounds like you want to be *taking care of yourself more*. What would be signs of that?

CLIENT: Not drinking. Keeping busy. The main thing is not worry about my husband. If I can do it living by myself, so can he.

CONSULTANT: Now, is that different for you to think that way?

CLIENT: Oh, yes! Because he got a car. He was not supposed to because we do not have the money. Oh, God, they cheated him. He was supposed to have five hundred dollars by the fifteenth of the month. I asked him where he was going to get the five hundred dollars. He just looked at me. I said to him, "Uh-huh." And I told him not to ask my son either.

So, when he got the papers, he tried to hide them from me and I said, "Where are you going to get five hundred dollars?"

Well, he got off his butt and got himself another job.

CONSULTANT: So, this is different for you to put your foot down.

CLIENT: Exactly.

CONSULTANT: Good for you. How'd you do it?

CLIENT: I don't know. He just got me so mad.

CONSULTANT: He's never made you mad before?

CLIENT: Oh, yes, but I just said, "This is too much. This has to stop!"

SUCCESS AND DIFFERENCE STORIES
IN SUCCEEDING MEETINGS

A couple came to see me quite upset about their relationship. The wife complained that they seemed to be stuck. In a recent conversation about whether to get married or not, they had begun to fight and the argument ended with both of them quite frustrated. He couldn't say what he wanted to do. He loved her and could not imagine being without her, but the thought of marriage put him into a panic. She thought she wanted to get married and wanted to talk to him. She wanted to move forward but she did not want to put some ultimatum on him.

When I asked what each of them wanted from coming to see me, she said, "I just want to see the relationship growing. I don't want to put an ultimatum or a deadline on this but I don't want to get into a rocking chair thing either where nothing happens."

When I asked him what he wanted, he said he thought he needed to figure out where he was. He said, "I guess I need to figure out where I'm at. I don't want to lose her and I think I am going to lose her if I don't marry her."

With some initial conversation about these desires, he told me how anguished he was about all this. He was very upset and was spending a great deal of time worrying and wondering what could be wrong with him that he could not know what he wanted to do. He figured there must be something wrong with him because other people get scared but they are able to get beyond it.

She talked about how time was ticking away for her and that she was now becoming concerned that she'd better make some decision.

They seemed to be thinking in black-and-white terms, either marriage or not marriage. I decided to ask a process question, i.e., "How would you know you were making progress toward some eventual decision? What would be some signs to you that you were making progress even if you did not immediately come up with an answer or decision?"

HER: I think I just need to see him more comfortable when I stay over at his house. He gets so upset and cannot sleep. He moves out onto the couch. I think I would just see him being more comfortable.

CONSULTANT: You'd see him being more comfortable. This would make a difference to you? (*I invite her to speak of the significance his comfort would make to her.*)

HER: I think, if he were more comfortable, I could do my thing. Right now, if he does not want to do something, then I usually don't. I guess I'd be doing things I want to do. Or if I didn't want to do something he wants, I just would not go. *I think I would just do more things on my own without feeling guilty.*

This appears to open up some possibilities for her. If before she thought she could not do things on her own for fear of the impact on him, she might now feel more permission to do things.

CONSULTANT: You'd like to be doing more things on your own, confident that that is okay or the thing to do. (*turning to him*) And what might be signs to you that you were confronting your fears or figuring things out?
HIM: Hmm, that is a tough one.
HER: (*She joins in.*) If we could just talk logically. Right now, we start to talk and then we usually run into something about his family and he gets quiet.
CONSULTANT: So, the two of you would be talking differently?
HER: I think it would be more comfortable.

Many avenues of inquiry come to mind. I could ask how it would make a difference if she or both of them were more comfortable. Would there be things they would be talking about that they do not now? Are there things that each of them would be doing that would be signs to each other that it was comfortable enough to proceed? What might be signs to them that it was okay to go a little further even if it was not totally comfortable?

CONSULTANT: What might be some signs even if it was not always comfortable?
HER: Well, for me, I think if I just *stayed calm and took a deep breath.*
CONsultant: That would be different for you to stay calm.

While I meant to merely mark this out as different, I regret saying this as she now expands, not on the difference or the staying calm, but her impatience. I wish I had merely said, "Tell me more about your wanting to stay calm," or "How are you thinking that your staying calm might make a difference?"

HER: Yes, usually, I just get too impatient. I figure we are right back in the same old place, he is not listening, he's saying the same old thing, and I walk away.

I turned to him as time was running out on our meeting. I want to hear what he might think were signs that the two of them were making progress.

HIM: I think if we could *talk logically and not get so angry about what we cannot change.* If we could just deal with it.

I am not sure if he is referring to him not being so angry with her or her with him, but time has run out. I take a break from the conversation and I go to another room to talk with myself about my thoughts and reactions. An explanation for the break and the notion of a reflecting disposition will be discussed in chapter ten. After a few minutes, I return to the two of them and share my thoughts.

CONSULTANT: I find myself really happy to hear about how you arrived at this point in your relationship. It sounds like the two of you really like each other a lot and really enjoy your time with each other.

Time has moved on and something must have been going right that you are now even considering a further step. I am glad to hear that you are attempting to talk about a further step even if it makes you uncomfortable, that you would think the relationship is that important to talk about a next step.

I hear that you would like some further movement at this time. It sounds like you assume that signs of movement might be your being more comfortable when she stays over, your talking differently with each other—perhaps a bit more calmly, your moving beyond the idea of changing the other, and your confronting some of your fears.

I am concerned that you might be looking for either him to be totally comfortable and for her to be totally free of guilt. If that is the case, I'm worried that if you do not see a total change, you will mistakenly think that no progress is being made at all. So, I am wondering what might tell you that you were making progress even if you were still sometimes scared, conversations were not totally comfortable, or you sometimes felt guilty about doing things on your own.

Neither of them had any immediate comment other than to nod their heads in understanding. Both said that they thought making another appointment would be helpful and we set it for a few weeks from that time.

When they returned, we chatted for a bit and then I asked what might have been any different or better since I saw them.

They looked at each other and said that things were about the same. I was concerned that, given that they were looking for change, things having been about the same might be construed as a setback or that things were worse.

When I asked if that meant that things were worse, they said, no, that things were not worse. I asked if they could explain. They said there was this thing that happened over at his sister's house. She said that they had been invited over to his sister's house for the christening of his sister's newborn. The party went from late afternoon on into the evening and she was beginning to get tired.

What she did was to approach him and say to him that she was tired and wanted to go home—this she did despite her fear that he would not want to leave and that he would be angry. She asked him if he could get a ride home with his brother. I asked if this was different for her to do. She said, "Yes." Normally, she would have stayed until late into the evening when he was ready to go home, even while becoming more resentful. I asked how she decided to say this to him and take that chance. She said, "I just figured that if we were getting serious, maybe it was time to take some risks."

I found myself feeling very excited about her deciding to take a risk that might make him uncomfortable but might be part of her doing something on her own. I was also very curious about what difference this may have made for him. I asked him what thoughts he had about what she was saying. He said that he was very glad that she spoke up. He was much happier having her leave rather than being angry all the way home.

I asked if there was anything else that had happened that would make them say that things were not worse.

They said they did have a fight recently about her picking on him. Rather than assuming that a fight is necessarily bad, I asked whether it was a helpful fight or a bad fight. They said they were not sure. He said that usually he is afraid to confront her about anything for fear that she will jump on him.

He went on to explain.

HIM: I was thinking she's on edge. I could understand that. She's been going through a lot at work and some other things with her family. But it just felt like anytime I was about to say something, she was real ready with a snappy comeback answer.

   All I had to say was, "I'm gonna do . . ." and she was ready to say, "Why are you doing it that way?"

   And I don't know how, but I just reached it. I figured, I gotta say something. I just couldn't take it anymore.

CONSULTANT: So, did she snap your head off or did it go differently?

HIM: At first she did. She didn't take kindly to my remarks. I mean we talked about it some and things are smoothed out now.

CONSULTANT: So, I am confused. How come this did not turn into a nasty thing or was this different for you to bring something up?

HIM: Usually, I wouldn't. I'm not usually one for confrontation. My family was never one for confrontation.

While his reluctance or fear of confrontation may stand out for him, I am more curious about something else. Given that he has just told me that he is not usually one for confrontation and that confrontation was apparently not practiced in his family, how did he decide to risk a confrontation this time?

CONSULTANT: So, given that your family was never one for confrontation, how did you decide to bring it up this time?

HIM: It was just really bugging me. I didn't know what was bugging her. Maybe she was just getting ready to say hit the road or what was on her mind.

CONSULTANT: I'm still curious though, because it sounds like in the past you would not have brought up something like this because you did not want to make things uncomfortable between you.

HIM: Yes, that's right.

CONSULTANT: So, how did you decide to take the risk and assert yourself?

HIM: I just figured things could not get any worse.

CONSULTANT: So, you brought this up and she did not take kindly to it. I am still wondering, though, how it did not turn into a nasty thing.

HER: I walked away from him. I went into the bedroom and straightened out a few things. Then, like we had talked about last time, I said to myself, "Before you go back out there in the living room and kick him to death, maybe you better *take a deep breath and cool down a bit.*" He has mentioned it before, but never come right out and said, "You are waiting to jump on me." I can't say I didn't see it coming.

So, when I went back out there, I said that I just didn't know what he wanted. He's made it clear he wants to do this kitchen project by himself, so why is he asking my opinion about his kitchen. (*They live separately.*)

I am struck by her taking a cue from the last meeting and how she decided to do something different. Rather than escalating the fight, she went into the bedroom, cooled down a bit and then returned to the discussion. It seemed to me that in the past she would have walked away and they would have remained angry or the fight would have escalated. It appears a different story is emerging, in which she is describing an active role.

CONSULTANT: So, this was different for him to say something this directly?

HER: Yes, I was surprised.

CONSULTANT: (*Because their voice tones are somewhat muted rather than excited, I wonder whether this difference they are describing is perceived by them as a success or something else. I am excited about the differences, but I am not sure they are.*) This was okay?

HER: Yes, I would rather have it out in the open than sit around and wonder.

CONSULTANT: Even if it makes you uncomfortable?

HER: The way I look at it, at least that is a *step forward*. Because most of the time I second-guess it, and if I say anything, then he says, "I don't want to get into it now."

The thing is *before*, if he had brought up something, if it was uncomfortable, we would both back off and not say anything. I had always thought that I don't want to say anything I'd regret.

So, this time I was shocked first off that he said anything.

I can barely contain my excitement. She is beginning to describe what they had presented as a fight as something different. She is storying this now as a "step forward" and different.

CONSULTANT: So, what did you think of his doing that?

HER: I was impressed.

CONSULTANT: What impresses you about his being assertive in this way?

HER: I like the fact that I can't walk on him!

I feel really touched by her saying this. It appears to be a very personal revelation about herself rather than about him. It makes me wonder if she has been looking for some evidence that she can depend on him and trust him to be strong.

HER: I think everybody sort of tests out the other person and I don't think I was deliberately trying to push him or test him. But with all the stress going on for me, I think I just let myself get out of hand.

CONSULTANT: So, does this make you more confident of him or the two of you?

HER: I think this gives me more hope of things changing for the better. If something comes up, he's not going to sit in a corner and not want to say anything. I think I did gain new respect for him.

CONSULTANT: (*I am very curious about what reflections or reactions he may have to what she has just said.*) Were you aware of this?

HIM: No, but she is right, this was different. I was more focused and I was more direct. I always used to be afraid that if I said something to someone, they would leave or not like me.

CONSULTANT: So, what do you make of it that she not only didn't leave but she likes you for doing it?

HIM: Yeah, that does shock me. Because it was not something I planned or thought out.

I am touched how this good experience has run totally against what he had expected. He had not expected himself to be assertive and he had not expected that she would respect him for being confrontive. I invite him to reflect on that.

CONSULTANT: So, what does it make you think about the relationship, that the two of you went through this, and she didn't leave and you worked it out?

HIM: I think it gives us something to look back at when we confront other issues. This is the first time that I took the lead when before I wouldn't have.

This dialogue is a good example of how storying success can take place in any time frame, even when clients do not initially see an event as any different or successful. The opportunity to inquire about differences or success may emerge as clients are talking about what they want in the future or in the midst of seeming pessimism. As consultants we want to keep a sensitive ear for differences within client stories. This couple had initially said when they came in that the previous two weeks had been about the same. However, the three of us have created two stories of success from the past couple weeks. In addition, both of them are stating that they see these stories as evidence of "movement."

This dialogue is also an example of the significance of thinking of story-ing rather than of facts and underlying meanings. By thinking of the three of us as storying, I am not interpreting their initial statement of sameness as a firm fact but merely as part of our conversation. I am also not thinking that below the surface of what they are talking about are underlying meanings that need to be dealt with. I could have assumed that he needed to talk about his fear of confrontation or fear of abandonment. Instead, we talk about the past in a fluid manner, as if there are many ways to story the events. The storying that took place obviously left them with some increased sense of agency and capability, being able to do something in situations where before they may have felt stuck.

In this chapter we have discussed how we and clients can inquire about and create different stories about their present or past. These inquiries encourage clients to story their present life in terms of some success and progress, which enables them to feel more of a sense of agency, more of a sense of getting what they want, and more optimism than before.

In the next chapter, we discuss how we invite other relevant voices into the conversation.

CHAPTER NINE

Inviting Other Voices into the Conversation

From Perceptual Frames to Conversation

As we have discussed in previous chapters, clients sometimes speak only of what they do *not* want or what they want to eliminate from their lives, such as alcohol or drug use. In interactional situations, clients often speak of what they want the other person *not* to do. Their only course of action at that time has been to try to get the other person to *stop* doing what they consider to be problematic behavior. The other person is also in a strange position, in that the options are either to defend the present behavior or to stop what the other finds so problematic. S/he is still in the dark as to what the client *does* want to happen. Sometimes, talking about what the client *does* want opens the conversation in a more positive direction.

The client very often begins by talking about what the other person will *not* be doing. Listen, wait for, and/or invite her or him to talk about what positive things will be happening that will tell her or him that the relationship is better. As we have mentioned before, the negative signs are helpful in hindsight, but positive indications expand the options and possibilities.

This opening of the conversation about positive changes the client is looking for in the relationship or the other person can be represented by the following questions:

What would be signs to you that your relationship was going more the way you want?

What would be different between the two of you?

What positive things would the other person be doing that would tell you the relationship was going better?

In interactional situations, clients frequently have *only* their own story. Even as we talk about the future and what they want to be happening, they many times have only their own view.

Sometimes, more possibilities can emerge and a different conversation can occur when we invite clients to speak from a different frame of reference, as if they were speaking for the other person in the situation. This is not a new technique. We discussed it in 1992. Gestalt therapy, Satir's conjoint therapy, psychodrama, neuro-linguistic programming, and other orientations over the years have asked clients to take on and act out the role of the other person in the situation. More recently, Karl Tomm has popularized the role play by using the concept and technique of speaking for the internalized other (Tomm, 1995). In these orientations, one usually takes on the role of the other in the problem situation. Experiencing the problematic situation in the other's role often develops empathy for the other. When we use the shift of frame of reference, we focus the role on the future. We ask the client to speak for the other person. What does the other person *want* and what would be *positive signs* to the other person of progress in the future? The point is to have the client not only develop empathy for the other but also contribute to a story of a successful future with the other person's voice.

A useful way to invite this reference change is to ask the following question:

Other-directed question: *What would your _____ (friend, spouse, partner, parent, teacher, employer, etc.) say would be signs to her or him that the relationship was going more the way s/he wanted?*

We also invite clients to speculate on how they would like to be different with this other person.

You-directed question: *How would **you** like to be different with this other person (spouse, partner, parent, etc.)?*

We may also invite them to respond to the other.

*Assuming your partner were to be different in the way that you want, how would **you** like to respond?*

The last invitation of another voice involves asking the client what reflections the other person might have about the discussion of the above answers. This conversation would be initiated by this question:

Reflective question: *If this other person were listening in on our conversation, what thoughts might s/he have? How might s/he say our conversation is making a difference to her/him?*

Below are some examples where some of the above questions facilitated more possibilities.

OTHER-DIRECTED AND YOU-DIRECTED INQUIRIES

The following conversation took place in a meeting with a couple. For the sake of brevity and clarity, we will present the unfolding story of just the husband.

CONSULTANT: Can you tell me what your goals are in coming here?

HUSBAND: We seem to be arguing a lot about stupid stuff. What was the last fight about? It was about who messed up the shaving cream in the bathroom. We just seem to be bickering all the time. If we could just get back to being happy again, where she wasn't quizzing me about all kinds of stuff.

CONSULTANT: Seems like the most frustrating fights are often about stupid things, aren't they?

HUSBAND: Yeah. If we could just be happy with each other again.

CONSULTANT: (*I am curious about what would tell him that the two of them were happy again.*) So, what would be some signs to you that the two of you were happy?

HUSBAND: Instead of spending the first three hours of the morning on the phone with her girlfriends, we might hook up and have coffee or that sort of thing. Our social life revolves around one or two dates in the future at her girlfriend's parties. Basically, I think she gives too much time to her girlfriends and a lot of time and energy is spent on them.

Not unlike a lot of people coming in for marriage counseling, he identifies the first noticeable sign as being a change in his wife. He describes what will not be happening, the time on the phone and the time spent talking and socializing with girlfriends, as well as what he hopes will be a positive sign to him, her having coffee with him. I ask him to expand on the positive sign.

CONSULTANT: So, rather than spending her time on the phone with her girlfriends, how would you like things to be?

HUSBAND: More time and energy spent on me.

CONSULTANT: Uh-huh. What would be signs of that happening?

HUSBAND: A little more attention on me, notice me in the morning whether I look good, bad or otherwise. Sometimes, I can look like a mad man. (*He laughs at himself.*)

CONSULTANT: So, she might be saying, "Hi." You might be having coffee together. Tell me what you would like about that. (*I am curious about how these changes by her would be significant to him.*)

HUSBAND: Well, there would be more attention on me. Right now we have a tight schedule and we don't see each other for days. It'd be nice to talk to each other.

CONSULTANT: (*I am still curious about how this attention would make a difference to him.*) How would this make a difference to you?

HUSBAND: I'd feel better about things. I would feel better about myself. Right now we are like strangers. We are doing our separate things. We don't do anything together. I work on the house. She is with her girlfriends or cleaning up.

   We don't have any organization. Right now, our only organization is who makes coffee in the morning. That's it. We don't have any set goals. We don't have any plans for the day.

CONSULTANT: (*I hear the significance for him of these changes by her as affecting how he wants to feel about himself and the two of them.*) So you don't want to feel like strangers. You want to feel better about you and better with her, working more together.

HUSBAND: Yeah.

The storying has now shifted away from what he does not want her to do, spending so much time with her girlfriends, to her paying more attention to him, to feeling better about himself and the two of them together. These latter themes have more of an open and positive feel about them and more potential for her to hear and for him to participate in.

   In hindsight, I wish I had inquired even more how these things would make a difference. I am curious about how he means that he would be feeling better about himself. In what way, would he feel better? Would he feel better about himself as a husband? If so, how?

   When he says that he doesn't want to be strangers, does that mean that he wants to be more connected with her—if so, in what way? Many times in working with couples, when we ask how the change in the other would make a difference to the first person, the answer is some variation of wanting to be closer or more connected.

   A little later in the meeting:

CONSULTANT: (*to husband, an other directed question*) If I were to ask her what would be signs to her that the relationship was going more the way she is hoping, what would she tell me?

HUSBAND: She would probably say that I would be picking up after myself, picking up my underwear off the floor and things like that.

CONSULTANT: Uh-huh.

HUSBAND: She'd also say that I'd be asking for her opinion or input about the house, maybe letting her know what I am thinking as well. (*They are in the process of renovating their house.*)

CONSULTANT: So, she would say that what might tell her that things were going better, would be seeing you picking up after yourself, asking for her input, or sharing with her what your plans or thoughts are.

   And how would she say these things would make a difference to her?

The significance of change question seems to fit here. He has stated two very specific things he thinks she is wanting and I am wondering what significance she might say they would have. This creates a means and ends distinction here. We are asking what difference his actions might lead to for her. His saying what he thinks she would say may have the added benefit of his developing some understanding and some empathy for her point of view.

HUSBAND: Hmm. She'd say it was respect. Respecting our space and respecting her opinion.

CONSULTANT: That is what she is looking for from you, respect. And to her way of thinking those would be some signs to her that you are respecting her. Even if you already respect her, this is what would do it for her? That's what you want as well—is for her to feel your respect for her?

HUSBAND: Right.

A little later:

CONSULTANT: (*you-directed question*) Can you say a little of how you would like to be different with her? Assuming she were to be doing some of the things you are hoping for, how would you like to be different with her?

HUSBAND: Well, I guess I would be listening to her questions rather than getting caught up in my stuff.

CONSULTANT: Really, you would like to listen to what she is asking about?

HUSBAND: Yeah, right.

CONSULTANT: Tell me more about that.

HUSBAND: I'd make the time and remind myself to listen to her.

CONSULTANT: How would you do that? It sounds like your schedules are pretty busy and there is a lot on your mind about this remodeling that you are doing.

HUSBAND: I would make a list in the morning of things I am going to do. My wife is a good list maker (*said jokingly and teasingly*) and she seems to get a lot of things done.

CONSULTANT: Sounds good, but it sounds like it would add another thing to what you are already doing.

HUSBAND: That's okay. It would be just a list in the morning or even before I go to bed at night. I read somewhere that if you make a list before you go to bed you get a better night's sleep.

CONSULTANT: I have heard the opposite of that—that if you start talking about things in bed, you get so stimulated you cannot sleep.

HUSBAND: No, this is before you go to bed and then you put it down. If I got myself better organized, that would give me more time to listen to her.

CONSULTANT: I see.

HUSBAND: I've been doing this the past couple of nights and it has been helpful.

CONSULTANT: You are already doing this?

This discussion of how he would like to be different with her has led into storying a recent success, his getting himself organized.

HUSBAND: Yeah, just a list. Then, I wake up and I make the calls, I am more organized and I feel better about myself. Then, I feel better about everything.

CONSULTANT: How'd you decide to do that?

HUSBAND: Well, it seems to work for her. She makes lists for herself. I thought we've been fighting a lot, so, I thought maybe this would help.

The tone in this conversation has changed. He started out talking about the fighting in somewhat defensive and angry tones. The mood changed as he talked about what he wants—more attention on him—and what she might see as signs of improvement. By the end he is volunteering how he would be different as well and how he is in fact already doing some positive things.

Given that this dialogue took place in a conjoint session, the advantage for her in listening in on our dialogue is that she can hear what he wants in positive terms. If she did not know what he wanted before, she now has options for herself that will make a difference to him. Frequently, we find that after so much conflict partners only know what the other person does *not* want. The other advantage for her is that she can hear him struggle with trying to say what he thinks she would answer to the questions of signs and significance to her. If he is mistaken, she can correct his impressions or add onto the list.

When I asked her, at the end of this conversation with him, what reflections she had about what was said, she responded that it was helpful to hear that he was serious about wanting to make things better and she was impressed that he was already trying to do some things. This softening of her tone, in addition to his tone change, left them both in a more open and less defensive posture than when they came in.

INVITING REFLECTIONS AS SOMEONE ELSE

A woman was concerned about her mother-in-law. She saw her mother-in-law as rather cold and unwelcoming. Beyond that she thought her mother-in-law attempted to take advantage of her. She also was concerned that her husband would not speak up for her to his mother in order to smooth things out.

CONSULTANT: So, you think your mother-in-law is rather uncaring and maybe jealous of you?

CLIENT: She sure seems to act that way.

CONSULTANT: And what would be some signs to you that she was more caring?

CLIENT: She would greet me with a hug and a kiss when I come over. She would call me once in a while. She never calls, I call all the time and she never says, "Thank you for calling."

She takes advantage of my having a car. The other day we were at the house and talking with my father-in-law and her sister. None of them have cars and they hate taking the bus. They were talking about how they needed to go Christmas shopping. My mother-in-law says to her sister, "We won't need to take the bus. Karen can take us." She never asked me or even looked at me.

If she cared, she would have said, "Maybe Karen could take us." Then she would have asked me. Or she could have asked me first before bringing it up. Or she could acknowledge that I do take them and that it is not always convenient for me.

CONSULTANT: Her affection, her calling, her asking and acknowledging, these are what you mean as signs to you that she cared and that things were going better?

CLIENT: Yes. That is what I would like. I am willing to do these things, but a little appreciation would go along way.

CONSULTANT: Would your mother-in-law say that she is concerned about anything between you?

As we discussed in chapter four, we are wondering "Who wants what?" in every consultation. Obviously, the client is very upset. However, is this a concern for the mother-in-law? If she thinks the mother-in-law is concerned, an other-directed question might be useful. We could ask: What might your mother-in-law say would be signs to her that things were better?

CLIENT: Hmm. I don't think so. I think she would say that things are fine.

Since the client thinks her mother-in-law is not concerned about the situation, the other-directed question would not be appropriate. However, I am curious about what reflections her mother-in-law might have about the present conversation. We generally do not ask this question until the conversation has developed to the point where some new story has developed. We might also ask this reflective question when what the client has said might be heard by the other in a different way. (Reflecting will be talked about more in the next chapter.)

CONSULTANT: So, if she were listening in our conversation, what would she think?

CLIENT: If she was listening in on what we have been talking about?

CONSULTANT: Yes.

CLIENT: Hmm. I think she would say she's surprised that I feel this way.

CONSULTANT: She would say she is surprised? How would she mean that?

CLIENT: (*reflectively and slowly*) She would say she's surprised because I've never said anything about it before. And she would probably say that she doesn't mean to offend me.

CONSULTANT: This would be surprising to her that you would feel this way. Sounds like she would have expected you to say something to her about it.

CLIENT: She would.

CONSULTANT: And would she be saying this defensively or would she be
really concerned that you are feeling unappreciated?

CLIENT: You know what, I think she really would be surprised and would
have wanted me to say something.

Since the mother-in-law is now mentioned as concerned, I am curious as
to what the mother-in-law would say would be indications to her that things
were better.

CONSULTANT: What would she say would be signs to her that something was
bothering you or that you wanted something from her?

CLIENT: I think she would say that I would have to just come out and say it.

CONSULTANT: This would be okay with her.

CLIENT: Yeah, that's her style.

In this example, as the client attempts to put herself in her mother-in-
law's shoes and answer for her, that is, reflecting on the conversation, the
client is surprised what she realizes. She realizes that the mother-in-law is
caring and would be concerned if she knew what was going on. One of the
possibilities that has opened up is talking to her mother-in-law, something
that she can do and that her mother-in-law might want her to.

A CONVERSATION LEADING TO A DISAPPOINTMENT

In a different example, a young man came in very upset about his mother.
He stated that his mother lived a few hours away in Wisconsin and that
recently they had had several serious fights on the phone. He was afraid that
she was going to close off from him and he did not want to see her isolated,
given that she was alone and getting older. He stated that he wanted be
more accommodating to her in order to keep harmony between them.

Signs to him of his being more accommodating would be that he would
be letting go of some of the sarcastic things she might say, he might manage
the flash points better by holding back on his anger, and he might be more
patient with her.

I asked him whether she was concerned about their relationship as well.
Again, as in the previous example, I am curious about "Who wants what?"
He said that he thought she was upset as well. Our guideline is that if the
other person is said to be concerned or wanting something, then s/he is part
of this grouping. The consultation membership is a grouping formed by the
emerging preferences and desires and includes the consultant who has
joined in by consenting to help. If the other person is said to want something,
then we ask the client to speak for her or him. In other words, we ask, "What
would _____ say would be signs to (her or him) that things were going
more the way (s/he) wants?" If the other is said to be unconcerned, we might

consider asking at some point, "If _____ were listening in on our conversation, what thoughts might (she or he) have?"

In this example, given that he thought she was concerned as well, I then asked what she might say would be signs to her that things were improving.

CONSULTANT: Given that you think she is upset, what do you think she would say would be signs to her that things were better between you?

CLIENT: What would she say?

CONSULTANT: Yes.

CLIENT: She would say that I would be returning her phone calls.

CONSULTANT: This is something she would say would make a difference to her?

CLIENT: Yes. She calls just about every day. Sometimes she calls because she cannot make a decision about whether to go out that day. I understand that she is afraid of the weather at her age. But she calls me at work and sometimes several times a day. She calls and wants to talk about my day as well.

CONSULTANT: This would be a sign to her.

CLIENT: Yes. She also would say that I would be changing my schedule when she comes in. She likes to come to the city by train. She wants me to meet her at the train and take her around. She also does not like to go out to dinner, so she wants me to cook and do things with her.

CONSULTANT: So let me see if I have all this. You are thinking you want to be more accommodating and patient with your mom, because you want to keep the relationship. You are also thinking that she would say that what she wants and what would be signs to her that things were better is that you would be returning her calls, picking her up, and doing things with her like dinner.

CLIENT: I think that's it pretty well.

CONSULTANT: And if your mom were listening in on this conversation, what would she say?

CLIENT: You know (*sadly*) I think my mother would say that I should be doing even more than that. She thinks that I am not doing nearly enough and that what I just told you would not be enough.

CONSULTANT: Hmm.

As the meeting continued, the client voiced his disappointed perception that no matter what he did his mother was going to say he was not doing enough. While discussing how a change in her expectations would make a difference to him, he began to talk about how he would not resent her and how he could relax a little, look after his own time, and not feel so guilty or sad about her. As he realized that she was not likely to change, he abandoned his idea of doing more for her and trying to accommodate. Instead, he speculated on how he would know that he was "drawing the line" with her in a way that felt caring to him.

Asking the client to reflect as the other person on what has been said can lead to the realization that the other person is concerned or that s/he is not. If the client realizes that the other is concerned, we can ask the other-directed question, "What would _____ say would be signs to her or him that things were better?" On the other hand, if the client realizes that the other person is not concerned about the situation, perhaps accepting that the other is not likely to change and making a change for oneself are the most viable options.

All four of these inquiries can be tools within a conversation to invite other voices into it. Where before there may have been only the voice of the client, inquiries to the voice of the other can produce dialogue. With only one voice there was monologue. With the mutual inquiry of both the client and the other, we can have dialogue and a new story.

Again the possible inquiries are:

1. What would be signs to you that your relationship was going more the way you want? What would be different between the two of you? What positive things would the other person be doing that would tell you the relationship was going better? These inquiries can invite the client's voice of the future with both negative and positive signs.
2. Other-directed question: What would your _____ (friend, spouse, partner, parent, teacher, employer, etc.) say would be signs to her or him that the relationship was going more the way s/he wants? This inquiry invites the voice of the other person in the future.
3. You-directed question: How would you like to be different with this other person (spouse, partner, parent, etc.)? Assuming your partner were to be different in the way that you want, how would you like to respond? These inquiries invite the client's voice of desire to be different within the relationship.
4. Reflecting on the conversation as the other: If this other person were here and listening in on our conversation, what do you think s/he would say? This inquiry invites the voice of reflection by the other on the present conversation.

This list is not exhaustive. There are other questions and other ways of expressing these questions that fit or can arise within the conversation. They can all invite a different and relevant voice into the conversation, even when it is just another voice of the client.

Let us now move onto two more dispositions of consultants, those of reflecting and encouraging.

CHAPTER TEN

Reflecting and Encouraging
From Feedback to Mutual Reflections

In chapter four, we discussed the metaphor of conversation and our use of the disposition being "curious with" as fitting within that metaphor. Being curious with includes the activities of (1) listening and affirming, (2) asking questions in order for the client to feel understood and for us to understand, and (3) furthering creative conversations. Within the conversation metaphor, reflecting and encouraging are two more dispositions and activities.

REFLECTING

By reflecting we mean several things. One way of understanding reflecting is a turning back, as a mirror does to our image. George Herbert Mead (1910, 1913), an early pragmatist, used this reflective idea when he proposed the idea of the social self. By this he meant that we as individuals learn about and form our images of ourselves as we perceive how others perceive or understand us. More recently, social constructionists Gergen (1994) and Shotter (1984) have articulated similar notions and have taken it one step further when they speak, respectively, of supplementation and joint action. They have shifted Mead's notion of the social construction of self to the realm of language and discussed how the meaning of what we say is reflected in how the listener responds and how the meaning continues to evolve. This perceptual notion of Mead's is now expanded into the realm of language and the joint construction of many meanings and selves.

For us reflecting is an activity that happens when we as consultants converse within ourselves or among ourselves as a team about what the client has said. It is also a mirroring back of what the client has said and a sharing of our internal conversations with the client. In addition, it includes the client's internal conversation about what is being said, clients' conversations between themselves if more than one, and conversations about the consultation that occur between clients and us.

The conceptual origins of a reflecting team go back to the late '70s and early '80s when the notions of second-order cybernetics and of a self-observing system were proposed. In first-order cybernetics, the focus was on the observed client system. This way of thinking was the basis for many of the information-system-based family therapy models: brief strategic therapy (Weakland et al., 1974), strategic therapy (Haley, 1976; Madanes, 1981), structural family therapy (Minuchin, 1978), systemic therapy (Selvini-Palazzoli et al., 1978), and neuro-linguistic programming (Bandler & Grinder, 1979). The therapist was assumed to be the expert observer of the client system, the family.

In second-order cybernetics, that of the self-observing system, no expert position was assumed. Instead, the members of the treatment system, that is, the therapist and the family together, observed themselves and their own observations. In practical terms this was a self-reflecting system and was described as second-order family therapy (Hoffman, 1983, 1985, 1993).

A reflective practice was first developed by Tom Andersen (1987, 1991) with his team members in Norway. Initially, they had practiced a systemic therapy and within that approach would talk, hypothesize, and strategize behind the mirror both during the interview and on the strategic break. This was similar to our taking a consultation break in our strategic practices. In both the systemic and various strategic approaches, the conversations would take place behind the mirror, outside of the clients' earshot. The conversations behind the mirror led to a unified message that was then delivered to the clients.

Andersen and his team decided to switch places with the clients at the time of the break. The team would gather in the consulting room and allow the clients to listen in on the conversation from behind the one-way mirror. They would then again switch places and the team would listen in as the therapist and clients reflected on what they had just heard. This was conceptualized as "dialogues and dialogues about the dialogues" (Andersen, 1987, 1991).

We have chosen the disposition and activity of reflecting for several reasons. The first is the experience of openness that it inspires. Years back, when we participated on strategic teams, we would gather behind the one-way mirror and strategize during the break in the session about what we wanted to say to the client and what intervention we wanted to give. The clients were not privy to this conversation. The therapist would then go in front of the mirror and deliver a crafted message, which often contained a paradoxical intervention. We did not engage with the clients about the message or the intervention because of our concern that if we talked with them about the paradoxical intervention the counterparadox would come unraveled. While these teams and interventions were very successful, when we participated on open teams or reflecting teams that others were using we experienced a refreshing feeling of openness.

The contrast between the strategic team and the reflecting team was brought home to us during a consultation by Harry Goolishian and Harlene Anderson many years ago. We were part of the team behind the mirror. Goolishian was in front of the mirror working as the therapist with a mother and her 13-year-old daughter. It seemed that every time Goolishian moved very far in conversing with mother, the daughter would interrupt in order to correct her mother, tell Goolishian the "real" story, or defend herself. On the other hand, as Goolishian would attempt to engage with the daughter, the mother appeared to do the same thing. The session was not going well. The result was that mother and daughter frequently broke into arguments and yelling, with Goolishian less and less able to conduct an open conversation. At that point, he stopped the session and suggested to mother and daughter that perhaps it would be helpful to talk with of them one at a time so that he could give each his undivided attention. He suggested that perhaps one of them could go behind the mirror, join the team, and listen in on the other's conversation.

Up to that point what he suggested did not sound all that different from what we were used to doing. We were used to seeing individual spouses or members of a family, one at a time, while the other went out into the waiting room. However, when Goolishian suggested that one of them go behind the mirror, we were taken aback. The daughter volunteered to go out of the room first. All of a sudden we were sitting behind the mirror with the 13-year-old daughter sitting next to us.

Several differences stood out to us with that experience. The first was that we found ourselves to be very quiet and reluctant to say anything behind the mirror, while we usually shared opinions freely. With the daughter sitting next to us, we were very self-conscious and aware of how much we talked about our clients behind the mirror.

Another difference was how intently this girl listened to the conversation between her mother and Goolishian. We conjectured that, without the opportunity to interrupt, she was free and open to listen and could hear the new material that was unfolding. On the other hand, we conjectured that the mother in front of the mirror was in a better position to engage with Goolishian. We imagined that without the interruptions both the mother and therapist were able to move beyond the initial presentation. As the conversation continued the mother was able to talk more about the fears and hopes that were influencing her choice to be strict and punitive with her daughter.

The third difference was how much more open the daughter was when she went back in front of the mirror, both about what she had just heard and also about what was going on for her.

Anderson and Goolishian explained their action of splitting up the session like that as a means to promote dialogue. As long as the mother and daughter were in the room together, creating dialogue was very difficult. When given the opportunity to talk to the therapist alone and later on to comment on what the other had said, they were both very open with each other. The result for us was a realization of a stark contrast between this way of working and our usual secretive actions in strategic teams. The advantages of the openness and facilitation of dialogue were impressive.

Adopting a reflective position as opposed to a strategic or evaluative one involved not just a difference of procedure but also a more open, public, and personal stance on the part of the professional. Harlene Anderson put it like this:

> Related to reflecting (and to sharing one's work in general) is the notion of being public—more readily revealing, more readily sharing out loud my private inner dialogues and monologues: my thoughts, prejudices, wonderings, speculations, questions, opinions, and fears. (1997, p. 102)

Part of the atmosphere of openness arises from what happens throughout the meeting. As the consultant takes the lead in being open and taking risks, clients will usually respond in kind.

Another reason for adopting the reflecting stance and a reflecting team was how it fit with postmodern ideas. In postmodern thinking, no particular idea or worldview is necessarily given more authority or privilege than another, including that of the consultant's. Freedman and Combs put it this way:

> By coming in front of the mirror and letting each of their individual voices be heard, reflecting team members put the postmodern notions of multiple perspectives, horizontal, collaborative relationships and transparency into action. (1996, p. 171)

James Griffith and Melissa Elliott Griffith speak of it as a political act that can have pragmatic consequences for the physically suffering patient.

> The use of the reflecting position in this sense is in essence a political act whose function is to distribute power among all the different voices in the discourse, dominant, and nondominant. The clinician thereby renounces a monopoly. . . . The gain for the clinician is the melding of perspectives that can bring forth a new reality in which the body of the patient is freed from its binds. (1994, p. 166)

In this instance they are speaking of not just a distribution of power but also the creation, through the sharing of reflections, of something new for the medical patient who is feeling the constraints of a binding narrative.

The final reason for adopting a reflecting disposition was that it fit conceptually with the conversational metaphor. In ordinary conversation, we listen, we acknowledge or reflect back what the other has said, we ask questions in order to understand, and we share our own thoughts. Reflecting is not a disposition and activity for just the consultant and not just for a reflecting break. We share our reflections within the conversation as well as at the reflecting break.

A reflection by the consultant within the meeting can be as simple as saying, "It sounds to me that what you want to be doing is taking care of yourself, but previously you thought taking care of yourself was being selfish." This is not a summary but a reflection of what the consultant has experienced in listening to the client.

Reflecting is an activity by the clients as well. We assume that clients are reflecting what they hear us say as well as what they hear each other say. Sometimes we invite the clients to reflect on what they imagine others would say. Other times we invite them to reflect on what they have heard others say within the meeting.

REFLECTING BY CLIENTS WITHIN THE CONVERSATION

Asking clients to reflect on what has already been said has been touched on in the previous chapter on inviting other voices. There we talked about how useful it can be to invite the client to take on the persona of someone else who is relevant to the situation of the desired change and reflect on the conversation. An example is a conversation with a young man concerned about conflicts with his father.

CLIENT: Every time I go home to visit my folks, this thing happens with my dad. When I tell him anything going on with me, he has to tell me how I'm doing it wrong—especially about my career. He always has a better way or has to point out how I am screwing up. How does he know? He was never a teacher.

CONSULTANT: Like he doesn't appreciate how difficult it can be?

CLIENT: Absolutely!

CONSULTANT: And you would like things to be different?

CLIENT: It would be nice to look forward to going home for a change. Now, I just avoid going home but then that isn't right either. Then my mother is upset with me too for not coming home. Then my dad is on me for hurting my mother by not coming home. Now, I just go home for the holidays and make excuses for not coming home other times.

Why can't he be excited for me sometimes or sympathetic with how hard it can be? I think he just never agreed with my career choice and still wants me to get into business. He never got as far as he wanted because he didn't have the education. He thinks with a college degree I should be making all kinds of money. I think he's still hoping I will give up and go back to graduate school.

Consultant: I see. He would like to see you making money or maybe the money he didn't.

Given our "Who wants what?" question, I am curious if his father is concerned about any of this as well. Perhaps if his father is concerned about the conflicts, I may be able to explore what his father wants different about the interactions through the use of some other-directed questions.

CONSULTANT: Is he concerned about this conflict between the two of you?
CLIENT: I think he's upset that I didn't listen to him. He can't figure the teacher thing.

Instead of my being able to explore the father's desires about their interactions, the conversation goes in another direction. The client tells the story of how his father wanted him to go into business or engineering. His father was very upset when he changed his major in school from business to education. For a long time he kept the change hidden from his parents. Given the fairly long history of disappointment and conflict about all this, I wonder what makes him still want things to be good or different with his father. Many people in his position would just give up the hope for approval or support.

CONSULTANT: So, given how things have been going, what makes you still want things different with him? You wouldn't be the first person to just write off his parent's opinion.
CLIENT: Because I would still like things to be okay when I go home. And his opinion still means a lot to me. I would like to think that he is proud of me and that he's happy for me, that I am ambitious in my own way. I am not going to abandon teaching just because that is not his idea of success. I just don't think he has any idea of what it means to me to work with kids or how much it hurts for him to be such an ass.
CONSULTANT: You've really been true to your own aspirations.
CLIENT: (*almost sadly*) Yes.
CONSULTANT: How have you stayed determined with all the difficulties?

The client expanded for a while how much he is committed to teaching despite the difficulties of the city education system. He is determined to stick it out this year and then check out alternative schools that would be closer to his idea of education. The tone of the conversation has changed from anger and disappointment with his father to pride about his career. Given that this story of pride is probably one that his father has not heard, I am curious about what his father might think of this. I ask the reflective question from chapter nine.

Consultant: So, I am wondering. If your dad were here what might he think of our conversation?

CLIENT: I don't know.

CONSULTANT: If he were talking only to me and being straight, what might he say?

CLIENT: Hmm. . . . To you, he might say that he's proud of my commitment. I suppose he would say that even if he doesn't like my choice.

CONSULTANT: What would he say that he likes about your commitment?

CLIENT: I think he respects that. I think he gets upset when he hears me complain about my job.

CONSULTANT: What would he say upsets him about your complaining?

CLIENT: I think he would say that he wants to know I am happy—sort of "If you're not going to make real money, you should at least be happy doing what you are doing."

CONSULTANT: So he has the wrong impression. He thinks maybe you are not happy with your choice.

The conversation progressed at this point around the idea that somehow his father had a misconception about him and his choice. Perhaps his father mistakenly thought that he was not happy or committed to his choice and was upset. We discussed what it would take for his father to have the *correct* impression, that he was very committed to teaching, that his complaining did not mean that he was not determined, and that he would like to have his father's appreciation of how difficult teaching can be.

In summary, the client initially vented his frustration about his father's reactions and then he was able to talk about what he would like—his relationship with his father to be less conflictual and more understanding. With the tone of the conversation having changed and his talking of his own pride and what he would like his father to appreciate and understand, the reflective question allowed him to understand his father's misconception of the client's complaining. This understanding led to exploring options of how he could show his father that his complaints were not all that was going on, that despite his complaints he was happy and committed to his career.

Another example of client reflecting is asking someone else in the meeting to offer her or his reflections on what the other has just said. This is not asking someone else to comment on whether they agree with what has just been said. To ask that would only invite evaluation and perhaps argument.

We sometimes introduce the idea of reflecting at the beginning of a meeting. If working with a couple, a family, or any grouping of two or more, we might say to a husband, for example, "I would like to listen to your wife describe how she would like things to be in the relationship for a while. I would like to ask you to listen, and then I will be interested in hearing your thoughts about what she said and how you would like things to be as well."

In situations where one person has a more difficult time listening to the other, we may ask that person to sit behind the mirror or merely a little way out of the conversational space and listen. This gives the listening person more of an opportunity to just listen. They may not be aware that their listening is what we think would be helpful. Some people come to consultation believing that consultants are supposed to be referees or mediators and so they begin talking to one another, unaware that we want them to listen and that the listening person will get her or his chance later.

What we are hoping for is that by our listening to one member of a family or couple for several minutes, several things can happen. The listened-to person will feel our listening and support and a new story can emerge, while the other member(s) may join in the listening in a different way. Rather than listening in order to judge whether they agree with what is said, perhaps they will find themselves caught up in the newness that has developed. Where before there had been arguing and disqualification of each other, we are hoping for listening and responding.

Here is an example of asking the members of the family to reflect on what has emerged between the consultant and one of the other family members. A mother had frantically called about her 15-year-old daughter. Mother came in for the appointment the next day with her daughter and the stepfather. Mother and stepfather began the family meeting by explaining that mother in her panic about how to manage her daughter had taken her to a hospital to be evaluated for drug abuse. The hospital had recommended a day treatment program for the next three weeks. The managed care company wanted a second opinion before it would authorize any treatment. The mother stated that she and her husband were at their wits' end. Her husband's view was that the daughter used to be a nice, well-behaved pre-teen, but had now become this sullen adolescent. According to him, she would stay out for days on end, she would come home smelling of alcohol, and her grades (which used to be B's and A's) were now C's and below. However, he stated what was the worst was that she yelled back at both her mother and him, causing escalating fights involving all three of them. "Perhaps," mother stated, "things have gotten worse because my mother is in the hospital close to death."

Throughout this conversation, our part, as consultants, was to listen to their ideas and ask questions of difference. Examples of the questions were: "How are your ideas about your daughter different from before?" "What effect do you think these ideas about your daughter have had on her?" "What difference do your ideas make to her perception of you and herself?" Mother did not know the answers to these questions but she hoped that her daughter missed the closeness that she and her daughter had before all this turned sour. Stepdad thought that their ideas about their daughter had no effect on her at all. In fact, he thought that his stepdaughter thought of no one but herself.

During this description by her parents, the daughter became more and more withdrawn. Occasionally, she would look up at her mother with eyes that said something to the effect of, "How could you say that about me?"

After both parents had voiced their opinions, I explained to them that I now wanted to hear their daughter's ideas about the situation. I explained that I would like them to listen to her and my conversation and pay particular attention to how they changed by listening to it.

I then asked the daughter what thoughts and ideas she had as she listened to her parents' conversation with me. She explained quite defensively that she was not as bad as they thought she was. She was not a bad kid. She explained her thoughts about school, her difficulties with homework, her feelings about her parents' "control" of her. Toward the end I thanked her for sharing all this information with me in front of her parents, especially since she did not want to come to the meeting in the first place. I then asked her if, like her parents, she would be willing to listen to the conversation that I was about to have with her parents. I asked if she would listen and take note of what differences she noticed in herself. She agreed.

I then turned to the parents and asked, "So what thoughts did you have as you listened to this conversation? How did it make a difference to you to hear our conversation?"

Mother spontaneously spoke first.

MOTHER: That is the most I have heard her talk and share since she was 12 years old!

CONSULTANT: How did what she and I talked about make a difference for you?

MOTHER: I could see that she is the same daughter that I once knew. (*Her breathing relaxes a bit.*) I thought I had lost her. She has just been so angry and she wouldn't talk about anything.

CONSULTANT: So, this was really different. Now that you think that she is still the daughter you knew before, what difference does or will that make to you?

MOTHER: Well . . . then, I guess I don't have to worry as much as I do. I can relax a little bit.

STEPFATHER: Well, I am not so sure about that. I was an adolescent once, into drugs and drinking. I think I have a pretty good idea about what she is into.

CONSULTANT: So, as you listened to your daughter and me talk what difference did the conversation make for you?

STEPFATHER: Well, I guess what I am saying is that I don't trust what she is saying, I think she is trying to snow-job us, particularly her mother, who is easier to fool.

CONSULTANT: So, how is what you are describing different from before?

STEPFATHER: It isn't.

I then turned to the daughter and asked her to reflect on her experience of my conversation with her parents. She said she knew that her stepdad did not trust her, but again, she said that she is not as bad as he thinks she is. I asked how that made a difference to her, to think that he did not trust her or that he thinks she is worse than she is. She said it made no difference to her—she didn't care. Even though she said she didn't care, I could not help but see in her eyes that she felt hurt by his words about her. She went on to describe her experience of trust between her and her friends, and between her and her parents. She spoke in detail about how her friends make decisions and what criteria they use to make "wise choices."

I then turned to the parents to have them reflect on this conversation.

CONSULTANT: First, I want to say how honored I feel that your daughter allowed me to have this very meaningful conversation with her, and to take the risk to have this conversation in front of the two of you. What thoughts did you have as you witnessed this privileged conversation?

STEPFATHER: You know, I am beginning to realize that maybe she is unhappy, not because of her mother, or me, or because of drugs or boys. But maybe she is unhappy because she is 15. When you are 15 you are unhappy.

CONSULTANT: Okay, that is an idea. How does thinking about her that way make a difference to you?

STEPFATHER: Well maybe then I don't have to do anything about it. Maybe I could just listen instead.

These conversations and reflections are examples of inviting members of the family to reflect on what newness may have developed in the conversation with the other family member. In this example, the mother seemed to be quite touched by hearing her daughter talk with the consultant. What she heard her daughter say seemed to reassure her that her daughter was in many ways still the daughter she knew earlier. She seemed to take this as a sign that she could relax a bit.

The daughter reflected on how untrue her stepfather's opinion was. She went on partly to defend herself but also to help the consultant understand that she was not a bad daughter. She trusted her friends and made good choices.

The stepfather's reflections the second time are different. Rather than hearing only the same old thing, he hears how she is unhappy and perhaps how that is not anybody's fault. His further inference is that if it is not his or her mother's fault, but just part of being a teenager, then perhaps he too can relax a bit. He seems less judgmental and more sympathetic with her unhappiness.

While we are stressing reflections, we would like to highlight that what the family members are reflecting on is the storying that is developing. As each family member talks about how s/he would like things to be, the ones who are listening hear previously unexpressed desires and vulnerabilities.

ENCOURAGING

As we think of ourselves as consultants with clients about their wants and preferences, we find that we strongly identify with their seeking changes in their life. Consequently, we want to say things like, "Good for you for doing that," "Keep on hanging in there," "Keep on doing what you're doing; it seems to be working," or "We are sorry about your setback; we hope this doesn't overly discourage you." These reactions are neither strategies nor detached interpretations about problems. Instead, they are genuine reactions to our clients' getting what they want in their lives. Encouraging seems to be a unique fit with our orientation to desires and wants.

The etymology of the term encourage is "to give heart to," which brings up images of standing behind people and supporting them as they look to the future and step forward. Encouraging also fits with the more collaborative space we are attempting to create. As opposed to praise or compliments, which can also be positive, encouragement is less evaluative and more a sharing of self. Readers familiar with our previous work (Walter & Peller, 1992) might note that this encouraging stance is a move away from compliments, messages, and formulaic tasks.

We share our encouragement both within the conversation and within our reflections at the break. Here is an example within the conversation: A couple comes in and reports that for the last two weeks there have been no fights and that actually they have been getting along.

CONSULTANT: For the last two weeks there have not been any fights?
WIFE: That's right. There have been differences, but when you have two small children to handle, differences are going to happen.
CONSULTANT: So, how did you do this?
WIFE: We just decided that we need time for just the two of us. So, we went out for dinner on Wednesday. He arranged for a sitter and we went out.
CONSULTANT: During the week! Good for you! (*enthusiastically*) How did you decide to do that?
HUSBAND: On the weekend, we are just too tired to go out. Besides, we just wanted time to talk. It wasn't like we had to have dinner, we just needed to be out of the house and away for a while from all the responsibilities.

Encouraging can include enthusiasm over success, cheerleading, acknowledgment of the difficulty of an accomplishment, and any other expression of support.

REFLECTIONS ARISING FROM THE THREE DISPOSITIONS

We assume that reflecting by consultants and teams flows from and is influenced by the overall metaphors of conversation and mutual inquiry of wants and desires. Thus, we assume that the consultant and team members will be involved in the same overall thinking of this approach and the dispositions of (1) being curious with the client, (2) being reflective, and (3) being encouraging with the client.

Being Curious with the Client

If one is being curious with the client as one listens in on the conversation between consultant and client, the team member will be involved in listening, affirming what the client is saying, and asking questions of her or himself out of curiosity. In other words, as a team member one would be involved in internal conversations that would acknowledge what the client and consultant are saying. The team member would also be asking her or himself questions that s/he would like to ask the client, the consultant, or both of them together. This does not imply creating questions that would then be phoned into the conversation in front of the mirror. This does not imply strategizing how the conversation should go. We do not phone in questions because we do not assume the questions are intended to gather important information. We do not want to break in on the conversation that is already taking place or initiate a conversation between the clients and those who are in the reflecting position. Questions are reflections of the listener's curiosity and, when expressed at the break, they are intended to invite a further conversation.

Listening and acknowledging to oneself what one is hearing, as well as asking oneself questions about what one is hearing, involve internal conversation as the team member listens. Monitoring and being aware of this conversation prepares one for being able to share these thoughts at the time of the reflecting break. This is no different from the internal conversations that the consultant has as s/he is sitting with the client.

Being curious is not just a passive disposition or activity; rather, it is also an inviting of different avenues of inquiry. A team member will respond to different parts of the conversation and will be curious and wanting to invite the conversation to take different directions. S/he shares these thoughts at the reflecting break.

In a recent meeting with a couple, Jane was talking with the couple about their wants, how each of them was hoping for the relationship to be different. The wife was complaining about how her husband was not making enough money in his business and about the drag this was placing on the family's ability to make ends meet. The husband appeared to John, who was behind an observation mirror, as caught between wanting to defend himself, on the one hand, and appearing very disappointed in himself, on the other. He complained about the lack of respect from his wife and daughter. What John found was that he (John) was acknowledging to himself how disappointing all this was and perhaps how sad it was. At the same time John became very interested in and curious about the husband's apparent desire to be respected. When it became time for the reflecting break, John shared the following with Jane in front of the mirror and in front of the couple:

> As I listened to the conversation, I thought to myself how sad it must be for him to think how disappointed his wife and daughter are with his financial problems. I also heard him say how difficult it was to know that they do not respect him about his income. However, as the conversation continued I became more aware of my curiosity about how much he wants their respect. Given how much this means to him as a husband and father, I thought of how much I would like that for him and began to wonder what might be some signs to him that they were becoming more respectful.

As this example shows, a team member acknowledges the storying as it unfolds and as the team member becomes an active listener. For John the unfolding story seemed to be one of not just the husband's sadness and disappointment but also of his desire for respect. John became became actively curious about the husband's desire for respect. A team member responds to her or his own curiosity about preferences that are developing and that could develop further.

In this example, the husband responded to this reflection by saying that, indeed, it was disappointing to not feel respected, and then he expanded on how much he wanted to gain his wife's and daughter's respect.

Being Reflective

As team members reflect on the conversation, they are also listening to and reflecting upon their own internal conversations. A team member will share her or his own changes relevant to the conversation that occurred as s/he listened to the client and consultant. These may be emotional changes or changes in thinking with regard to the client or the client's situation. Very often as the conversation progresses toward successes, the team members experience a growing excitement for the client. Other times these changes are influenced by the experience the team member brings to the conversation.

In a recent consultation that I (John) was doing at a family service center, I was asked to be the consultant for the therapist and family. The family members were a young man of 18, his father, and his mother. The young man had been fired from his job for substance abuse and had ruined any hopes he might have had for joining the military and having a military career. His parents were extremely upset. His father had been a military man himself and had hopes for his son's military future. However, given what his son had done, he had become quite punitive and critical. His mother was shocked and upset. During the initial conversation, the son talked of his decision since the firing to make some changes for himself and how he was checking out other job situations so that he could go to school for a while. In front of the mirror, I was quite taken by this son's decision and touched by his love for his father. At the same time I was avoiding conversation with the father because I was afraid that he would again break into a tirade of anger.

When it came time for the reflecting break, the family went behind the mirror as I talked with the team members who had been listening in. I shared my excitement for the young man and how he was deciding to respond to this dramatic setback in his life. At the same time, one of the men on the team began sharing how his own disappointment with his own son had affected him. He began to share not only his disappointment at the time of the "screw-ups" his son had repeated over and over, but also how difficult it was for him to maintain faith in his son at that time. He spoke of how his disappointment got between him and his son, when what he wanted was to keep faith in his son and for his son to know that.

When the family returned and I asked for their reactions and thoughts, the father, instead of being angry, said how much he appreciated the fellow father's expression of not just how difficult it was but how much he wanted to keep faith. He felt comforted by knowing he was not the only one who was struggling but also by hearing another father talk about his desire to keep faith in his son. He went on to say how he *did* have faith and hope in his son and how he wanted his son to know that.

I was quite touched by the acknowledgment and solidarity that had been created between the two fathers. I had not thought at that time how much the father would want to have faith and hope in his son. It made me very grateful for this team member's sharing. I was also very grateful for the generativity of multiple conversations and reflections that can take place with a team.

This is a good example not only of a team member's sharing his observations but also of an observation arising from within his own experience. More than the observation that his distress was normal, what seemed helpful for the father was hearing the other father's own story of struggle and, more importantly, his desire to keep faith in his son.

Being Encouraging with the Client

We have already discussed the sharing of encouragement by the consultant within the conversation. Team members also respond with an encouraging disposition. Behind the mirror, team members note actions or ideas that the client is discussing that they want to encourage at the reflecting break.

A REFLECTING BREAK WITH A TEAM

While reflecting is a continuing activity of the consultant, the client, and/or a team, we formally offer our reflections during a reflecting break in the meeting. We have not formalized the reflecting break as having to take place at any particular time. We usually take the break toward the end of the meeting time, so that the consultant or team can offer reflections on what has already been discussed and still reserve time for the client to reflect on the reflections. Sometimes we break earlier if the conversation seems to be bogged down and the team has reflections on the process of what is not happening or many questions for the client.

During this break, the team members come into the room and converse in front of the clients. They share with each other what they were thinking as they listened to the initial conversation and/or reflect on what some other team member has already said. Sometimes the consultant may join this conversation, but usually s/he listens to the team along with the client. This conversation in front of the client is not directed toward the client. This is not a feedback report to the client. The client listens in on this conversation between members without being part of it.

Team members generally try during that time to share with each other what changes took place *for them* as they listened to the conversation. In other words, the conversation is not the sharing of evaluations of the client or evaluations of what was heard but more a sharing of what happened or changed in each member's own internal thinking and experience as s/he listened. As they share their thoughts and what has happened with them during the conversation, their language takes on the form of "I" messages rather than the language of evaluation or prescription. They may also share what in their own experience influences what they are saying.

You can imagine that, given the orientation to client wants and desires and given the creative direction of most of the meetings, many of the thoughts expressed are ones of excitement about already occurring changes, encouragement of new ideas or preferences, and a sharing of hopefulness. This does not mean that the only thoughts that are shared are positive and that they are always hopeful and positively focused. This would be positive for the sake of being positive, i.e., positive-forced. Instead, conversation inspires a sharing of enthusiasm for new ideas and successes, caution when warranted, doubts and fears when these are our reactions, as well as further curiosity or wonderment.

A middle-aged man who came in recently was worried that he was not being productive. This was his second meeting, and initially he said that he was doing better since the last time. He stated that he was feeling better. He had been rather worried about a bout of bronchitis, given that he had only one lung. However, now that he was feeling better he was worried about whether he was being productive. He was attempting to write a book and this was his first attempt at writing. He stated that he was confused about whether his sleeping late in the morning was just his usual style or whether he was in some way procrastinating on his work.

When asked what he wanted from coming to see us, he said that he thought maybe he needed more willpower and that he wanted to be productive for himself and his family. He had been feeling down, as he thought that he had gotten off track.

One of the signs of being productive would be his getting up in the morning before 11. Eleven was his cut-off time between being productive and procrastinating. He did not need to get up much earlier than 11 because he knew his rhythm was typically to stay up late at night and then rise relatively late in the morning.

Other signs would be his taking some initiative. Instead of leaving all the booking for his band up to the manager, he would be making some calls as well. The significance of this would be that he would feel that he was not being so passive and taking the easy way out. He said that he had a recognized name within music in the clubs of the area and so it would not be out of bounds for him to make some calls. Otherwise, he would be just waiting for the manager to have the time to get something going and feeling frustrated that he was not playing music.

He then went on to tell a story of how after his surgery, in which his lung was removed, some friends had organized a benefit for him. They had invited a number of people to a club to honor what he had contributed as far as music and to acknowledge his surviving the surgery. He said it was an "It's a Wonderful Life" type experience. It was a little like being at his own funeral, he said, as he listened to all these people talk about all that he had done. He said he even got up on stage and sang with his remaining lung.

"I still have not taken the whole experience in yet," he said. I asked, "If you had taken it in, how would it make a difference?" He said that the experience meant that he *had* been productive, that he *had* touched people, lots of people, and that it validated his having gone through a lot of crap and tough times.

He ended the conversation by saying that this past week he had been taking his daughter to work and had been getting up earlier in the morning. He also had gathered more material together for his book. His last thought was that maybe he was coming out of the recovery period from his surgery and was now getting into things.

The Reflecting Break

The three team members came into the room from behind the observation mirror. They sat in a circle talking with one another in front of the consultant and client, who listened in on the conversation. The conversation went like this:

FIRST MEMBER: I was so impressed with what he has achieved. I can't sing; I cannot stand my voice. So, I envy his singing. There is a story about the singer without a song, but he's a singer without a lung. Yet, he is still out there singing his song.

SECOND MEMBER: I heard that, too, and about his wanting to write. I resonated with his worries about being productive. I think it is confusing for me sometimes whether a lack of progress is due to a lack of discipline. I can get into a whole thing about that. But, I think to myself on those days when I don't get started as early as I have set my mind to, that the important thing is to keep my mind on the prize. Otherwise, I could get myself into a funk thinking that, because I did not do all I was supposed to, that must mean that I have failed. Then I would not do anything.

At the same time, I heard him say that this past week he has been getting up and taking his daughter to work rather than going back to bed. He's also been gathering material for his writing. It sounds to me like he is preparing himself and getting himself ready for more work. It sounds like he is maybe breaking himself in like an athlete who is getting himself into shape again. I just wonder still how he decided to do these things this past week.

THIRD MEMBER: I was wondering that too. He had been sick for quite some time. I found myself thinking of him as someone who likes to share himself with others—maybe through his singing, maybe through writing or some other way. It seems like this illness has been a distraction from his usual mode of sharing himself with others. I was thinking and wondering how frustrating it must be for him not to be able to share of himself like he's used to. And I hear that he has a strong desire to get back in the action. I wonder if this thinking of acting like an agent for the band isn't part of that desire.

SECOND MEMBER: My worry is that he would now somehow think that because of his missing lung or his not being productive like a nine-to-five person that he would think he is defective or failing. Sounds to me like he just has his own way.

FIRST MEMBER: Yeah, I hear a lot of pride in him and I hear this benefit event, not as a funeral but as a beginning.

The reflecting team returned behind the mirror and the consultant turned to the client.

CONSULTANT: So, what stood out to you?

CLIENT: Well, it was nice. It is nice to know that I am not the only one who struggles with their guidelines of how to work. Everyone does have his own way and I should not get crazy if I do not always do it on a schedule everyday. The idea is to stay with it and think about what I want to share.

CONSULTANT: Other things stood out?

CLIENT: Well, they are right. This is not a funeral for me, this is not an ending *(tearfully)*. My illness is not an ending. Thank God, I can still sing and bring my energy to people. I am not a singer without a song. My song comes naturally and I have had the chance to see how much people like it.

The reflections of the team seemed to flow from the initial conversation. In the initial conversation the consultant discussed what the client wanted, his being more productive for himself and his family. They further discussed what would be signs to him that he was being more productive and that things were going more the way he wanted. The signs he mentioned were that he would be getting up earlier in the morning. He also would be taking more initiative, for example, making calls to arrange more work for his band. This led to a story of how friends of his had given a benefit party for him to cover some of his medical bills. It had been a huge success, with many people attending and honoring him by talking about all the things that he had done. He said this quite emotionally and reflected that the experience had not all sunk in. When asked how this would make a difference, he had talked of how confirming it would be for him to take it all in, realize that he had been productive, and that he had touched people.

The reflections of the team followed his preference to be more productive. Part of the reflection supported his being active despite his surgery and removal of his lung. Another part acknowledged his recent initiatives regarding getting up earlier and his thinking of taking on more. One member spoke of his own difficulties in reassuring himself that he is productive and his difficulties in keeping his focus on his writing goal.

Still another member of the team offered a different view, which is that all of this seems to be part of his desire to share of himself, and the thread that continued seemed to be that each person has his own way of being productive and sharing.

He seemed to feel that what he had said was confirmed and to take heart in the encouragement to continue to "prepare himself" as an athlete would and to continue to share of himself.

These reflections seem to include all of the dispositions we have discussed. The team members listened to what the client and consultant had been discussing in an affirmative and curious manner. They heard this man's desire not only to be productive but also to be confirmed as having made a difference to people. The team members also shared their experience of the conversation. The first member shared his respect for the man singing with only one lung and his envy of how the client is singing his song. The second member shared some of his own difficulties and also encouraged the client to keep his goal in mind and continue his recent efforts to get himself "in shape." The second member shared his continuing wonderment of how the client decided to make these efforts of the past week, as if inviting the client to engage that question as well. The third member shared his experience of the conversation. He shared that the client seemed like someone who likes to share himself in song, music, or writing. His experience is that the client must be frustrated with how this recent surgery has distracted him from his desire. He also expressed his wonder about the recent changes by the client.

While the reflecting break is a conversation between the team members and therefore a spontaneous interaction, the dispositions of team members are obvious. This reflective conversation was not a rehearsed or packaged delivery of a previously prepared message. There was no predetermined format. What were shared in the conversation were the team members' changes in thinking and experience behind the mirror, including the dispositions of being curious with the client about what he wants, the inviting of further inquiry, the sharing not only of the team members' reactions but also of how his experience resonated with their own experiences outside of the meeting, and finally the encouragement. These dispositions are all part of the orientation of personal consultation.

The three dispositions of being "curious with," being reflective, and being encouraging are part of the consultant's way of being with the client and of the team members' attitudes behind the mirror and within the reflecting break.

REFLECTING WHEN WORKING ALONE

When working alone, we take a short break to converse within ourselves about what we have heard and what happened for us during the meeting. We may leave the room or just turn away for a short time to collect our thoughts or have a conversation with ourselves. We then share with the client those conversations we are having within ourselves and invite her/his reactions or comments or further thoughts. We generally ask, "I am curious about what thoughts you have about what I shared with you or what we have talked about. What may have been different or interesting?"

An example involves a young man who during our first consultation talked of a recent crisis due to his drinking and separation from his wife. He was now living with his mother and had recently been fired from his job. He and his wife used to spend almost all their nonworking hours in bars or in front of the TV at home drinking on into the night. He described blacking out many times in public places, both with his wife and alone. More than once he had found himself home or at his doorstep without knowing how he got there. He and his wife separated because he had been fired over her. They worked together and he had covered for his wife's absence or lateness many times. His boss had recently found out about his lying and fired him. Over the fight about this with his wife, he had chosen to move out.

As we talked about what he wanted from coming to the consultation, he said that instead of being sucked in by guilt when he talked with his wife, he wanted to stand up to her, change his drinking, and keep a clear head. He had gone two and a half weeks without going to a bar and he had not been drinking while staying at his mother's. But without alcohol, he found himself crying much of the time, as if all these emotions he never thought he had were rushing out. Further signs to him of being "clear-headed," another thing he wanted, would be his going for job interviews, spending time alone and with his mom, and not trying to rescue his wife.

The consultant reflections went like this:

CONSULTANT: Good for you for coming in (*affirming his doing something for himself and encouraging his efforts*). I cannot imagine what the last two weeks have been like for you—losing your job, your landlord threatening to kick you out, having to ask your mother for help. I find myself wondering how you are deciding to think about yourself and seek clarity for yourself with all this going on. As you said, you could be doing all those destructive things or things that were making you feel worse.

So, I am finding myself feeling good for you as you talk about doing things on your own, crying and feeling the pain of things, and doing the resum and job interview thing. It all sounds so painful and yet you are finding yourself doing some good for yourself in the midst of it all. I am just wondering still how you are deciding to face some of this and take the actions you are.

CLIENT: Yeah, it has been bad. I just didn't think I could go that low. But you are right, I got to keep on thinking of the "clarity." It is a little easier with my wife mad at me, but I got to think about me.

This brief interchange was somewhat encouraging of the recent changes and decisions he has made. The initial conversation had authored an unfolding preference for wanting to look after himself and keep his head clear. At the same time, what I found myself wondering about was what it must take for him to come to terms with all this and decide to do some of what he has. In keeping with the notion of reflections being a sharing of self rather than an assessment by an expert, I shared my reactions to his recent changes and my amazement and curiosity about how he was doing it.

While this exchange was encouraging and focused on his positive desires and preference, other conversations, and therefore other reflections, are not so positive or do not build on recent changes.

A young woman talked about her ambivalence and conflicts about her marriage. She had married this man several years ago and had gone through a very rough period when he had been using cocaine heavily. She had insisted that he stop drugging, and through that rough time he had stopped. He was now going to twelve-step meetings and had been sober for several years.

However, the cessation of his drugging had not made things all better. Now that he was sober, she was even more aware of the differences in their hopes and dreams for the future. He was a construction worker and loved to work with his hands. He was quite happy with that, but this was not what she had expected. She had expected that he was going to return to school and finish college. She found that, while he had a curious mind, he was not really interested in books or in art, two of her passionate interests. Given that his income was sporadic and never very much, she was wondering whether she was selling herself short. The final area of conflict was that they had no friends together as a couple. He had friends whom he worked with, and she had her friends.

On the other hand, they had been together for a long time and she was not sure that she would be any happier if she left him. In our meetings we discussed how she might make herself happy on her own and then see what difference that made. We also talked about her pretending she were happy with him to see what difference that would make in terms of her actions and his responses. None of these actions seemed to produce enough of a difference to help her decide upon some immediate action. She was afraid to talk to him about any of this for fear the discussion would precipitate some action on his part. Perhaps he would leave and then she would be alone.

My reflections to her were these:

> I am feeling really bad for you. It seems that you have been very unhappy with your marriage and it seems like a shame that there is nothing that strongly tips the scales to help you determine what to do. I suppose in some ways the safest thing to do at this time is just to leave things as they are. At the same time, I hear that you are very much aware of how you want something more in your relationship. I understand that you are reluctant to talk to him about this and share the responsibility for some decision because of your fear of his reaction. However, I worry that this leaves you tremendously lonely.

Her response was that she did feel very lonely and alone despite being married. She acknowledged that she felt very lonely and sad. She said she needed to think about this awhile.

While we naively wish that all our consultations would lead to immediate happy endings, this is not always the case. Sometimes, as this example illustrates, the client experiences some affirmation of her or his experience, but she appears cautious about this situation and wants to think about what she wants to do.

SUGGESTIONS

When we were committed to strategic and problem-solving approaches, we had a list of tasks and interventions that we assigned to our clients. Each task or intervention resulted from the problem that was presented. If clients complained of being obsessive, we suggested that they spend some time doing quality thinking. We suggested that they think about the problem every day for a prescribed amount of time and that they ask a different kind of question; rather than asking, "Why was the problem happening?", ask "What was worth thinking about?" This created a distinction between useful and non-useful thinking.

As we have moved to inquiries and conversations around wants and preferences, these tasks have become less significant. Since we do not conceptualize our work as moving the client from a problem state to a solution state, we no longer think within the language of intervention. We think of ourselves as involved in facilitating creative inquiries and conversations and assume that preferences and possibilities are developing and evolving within those conversations.

What we have found useful is to encourage clients to look for and take note of any times when things go more to their liking. As the conversation has been about preferences, wants, successes, or recoveries from setbacks, we encourage clients between meetings to look for any times when things go more the way the way they want. If you remember the "beige" exercise (see p. 91), this suggestion will make even more sense to you.

When clients come to consultation, the beige of their problem is prominent in their foreground, all they experience and see. As we acknowledge the beige and then ask what they want, they might say, "I would like some variety of color in my life, a little red, a little green, or a little blue." Since they have begun to converse about their preferences, a variety of colors, we suggest that they go look for those colors. In other words, at the end of the meeting we suggest that clients take notice of times when things are going more the way they want.

This is an extension of the formula first-session task from solution-focused brief therapy. Within that model, the task was phrased like this:

> Between now and the next time we meet, we (I) would like you to observe, so that you can describe to us (me) next time, what happens in your (pick one: family, life, marriage, relationship) that you want to continue to have happen. (de Shazer & Molnar, 1984, p. 298)

This task was used to turn clients' attention away from the problems and toward solutions or goals. It was also used to help clients who had only vague descriptions of what they wanted to develop more specifics. Extending the spirit of this task, we support clients' turning their attention to their wants and preferences. We assume that they will notice some of the preferences already discussed in the consultation meeting, as well as others that might not have been discussed yet.

We generally suggest at the end of the meeting or at the time of our reflecting break that it might be helpful for them to take notice of any times when things go more the way they want. Our intention is to support the conversation around preferences and possibilities and the idea that when clients look for and call attention to what they want, they are more likely to find it. Also, by focusing on what they want in a positive fashion rather than focusing on what they are trying to eliminate, they have a better chance of getting what they want. We make this suggestion not just at the initial meeting but throughout the course of the meetings.

We have no causal hypothesis or prediction about this. Sometimes, clients leave meetings with more awareness of their wants and preferences, and they then do something different from before. Others leave the meeting with more awareness of and sensitivity to what they want and then notice those occasions when what they want happens.

In the next chapter we describe several meetings with a client, so that you can get a sense of how this all fits together.

CHAPTER ELEVEN

A Personal Consultation from Beginning to End

Conversing about Trust and Clear-headedness

L et's look at one consultation in its entirety.
      The questions that we have discussed as helpful tools for the development of preferences and possibilities are italicized to highlight not only how these questions can be useful but also how they can arise throughout the conversations. In highlighting these questions, we realize there is a danger that you will think that the questions make the conversation. That, of course, is not the case. Inquiry takes place within conversation and arises from within conversation. This orientation is about conversation, not about questions.

We had a difficult time selecting which consultation to present. There were others that were briefer, or that might have seemed more challenging, or where the change seemed more dramatic. We chose this one because it shows how change does not always go smoothly or neat and orderly. It also shows how circumstances can impinge on the number and frequency of meetings.

FIRST MEETING

A young woman of 27 came to see me. I told her that I would like to talk with her for about 45 minutes about what she wanted, what changes she might be hoping for and anything else she might want to talk over. At the end of 45 minutes I would take a short break and leave the room to think over what she had said. Then I would rejoin her, share with her whatever thoughts or ideas I had, and then discuss with her whatever thoughts or reactions she might have.

She acknowledged what I said, and then I asked her *what she wanted from coming in.*

She said that she had separated from her husband and that she was going through a divorce. Her husband had her little girl, and her being apart from her daughter was very hard. Then she said:

CLIENT: I want to find out why I turn to drugs rather than deal directly with my problems and things.

What I hear and reflect is a beginning statement of desire, her wanting to deal directly with her problems and things.

CONSULTANT: You want to be dealing directly with your problems?

CLIENT: Yes, but I don't deal with them. I'd rather get high. I know I can't have them. I have to quit completely.

CONSULTANT: What makes you say that, that you have to go completely without?

CLIENT: Because I went through a rehab before for alcohol. After a while, I thought I could have one drink or smoke a little pot. But I can't, I went right back into it and then did other drugs.

She continued her story of having gone through the rehab and how she also started taking prescription painkillers. In the midst of this story she said that she went a year without any drugs before abusing the painkillers. She said that when she found out she was pregnant, she stopped all drugs and continued even after the baby was born. I acknowledged this as something different and as something she would like to get back to. Then, because I wondered if there was more that she wanted beyond dealing directly with her problems, not doing drugs, and having an answer for why she turns to them, I asked:

CONSULTANT: So, is there more that you are looking for?

CLIENT: I just want to get back to a normal life, have my daughter back living with me, get back to work, and have some kind of normal structure I haven't had for several months.

CONSULTANT: This is different for you to be apart from your daughter?

CLIENT: (*with some anger in her voice toward her separated husband*) Yes, it's different to be apart from my daughter, to be out of my home, not to be working. You know, it's like in the last six months everything is just completely changed.

CONSULTANT: Oh, (*sadly*) I'm sorry you are having to go through all that.

This portion was quoted in chapter four as an example of listening and acknowledging client concerns. In general, we accept and acknowledge client statements of concerns or problems. Rather than trying to unpack or deconstruct a client's statement of a problem or complaint, we merely accept it and eventually move on to a conversation of what they want or how they would like things to be. This is consistent with our preference rather than problem/solution orientation.

CLIENT: Not only that, but you know everyone dreams of having nothing to do but, let me tell you, that gets real slow and boring real quick.

She continued to describe her frustration with her husband and the recent story of her separating. What becomes curious for me is how, given frustrating and bad things have been going, she is now choosing to make such a change.

CONSULTANT: In the midst of all this, you decided to stop the drugs?
CLIENT: I want to cope on my own.
CONSULTANT: Tell me more about that.
CLIENT: I have to quit. I've seen what it's done to others and it seems I'm headed that way. I've lost my daughter and my house. I'm not as far as others, but I'm going that way.
CONSULTANT: That's where you saw yourself going and you want to get your daughter back.

Here is an example of where a preference orientation seems to make more sense than a well-specified goal orientation. She has mentioned several things that she wants. She has mentioned quitting drugs, getting her daughter back, having a job and a normal life. Rather than pursuing each one of these in an instrumental or problem-solving fashion, we converse with her about the significance of these preferences and how she will know they are happening as a way to open up the conversation and possibilities. If we were to adopt an instrumental problem-solving orientation, we would be asking which of these she wanted to start with and how she could make each of these happen. We would also attempt to make each "goal" well specified.

The thread of the conversation seems to be that she wants to quit drugs and deal with her problems directly. She seems to think that knowing why she takes them would be helpful. Furthermore, she wants to cope on her own and get her daughter back. She sounds very pained by the absence of her daughter.

CLIENT: I want to quit. My husband thinks I won't quit.
CONSULTANT: You want to prove him wrong.
CLIENT: Not really, I'm just afraid that I will lose contact with my daughter.
CONSULTANT: What is it about your daughter that makes you want to do this?
CLIENT: I let her down. (*She begins to cry.*) I want to make it up to her.
CONSULTANT: (*after some silence*) What makes you want to do that for her?
CLIENT: I love her. I want her to trust me and depend on me. I can see it in her eyes that she wants to, but I can see her doubts. I want her to feel secure with me.

Asking this question, "What makes you want to?" allows the client to amplify and expand the context and reasons. The story development becomes even more compelling for me as she explains and describes further how she is choosing to pursue these changes.

CONSULTANT: Hmm. So, *what are you thinking would be signs to her* that she can trust you and feel a bit more secure?

She has begun to talk about changing in her drug use as a possible means to changing her relationship with her daughter or as part of her keeping contact with her daughter. Since she said that she wants her daughter to trust her, I am curious about what *her daughter* will notice from her point of view that would contribute to her trusting. The other-directed question seems appropriate.

CLIENT: If I followed through, came on time.
CONSULTANT: Anything else?
CLIENT: That's the biggest. This is something I have to work on. I'm always late.
CONSULTANT: *Anything else that would be a sign to her?*
CLIENT: Doing what I say I'm going to do. You know, if I say I'm going to pick her up at 7, be there at 7. Now, sometimes it's 7:30, sometimes not at all.
CONSULTANT: What makes you look forward to that?
CLIENT: Just to see her excitement and not hear that little bit of doubt in her voice when we are on the phone.

She goes on talking more about what a good kid her daughter is and how she wants to do right by her.

CONSULTANT: *What might be other signs to you that things are getting better?*
CLIENT: If I wasn't feeling depressed. I don't share with anyone. I am just like my mother. We both keep everything in. My husband thought I was nuts taking a vacation with my mother one time. He says, "How will you last more than a half-hour, neither of you can talk about yourselves?" But I think I can.
CONSULTANT: What makes you want to share with someone else?
CLIENT: Because it is very lonely right now.

In the remainder of the meeting she talked about what it had been like to go the past several days without any drugs. She said it helped that there was no one around who was doing any and it helped that she did not know anyone whom she could buy some from. On the other hand, she said that she could easily find someone, so maybe the fact that there was not anyone around was not as important. This made me curious about how she had not sought out drugs.

She also told me the story of how she wanted to get high last night after a fight with her mother. As upset as she was, she went to bed instead. Her only explanation for her decision to go to bed rather than go out and find some cocaine was that she just had to stay away from it.

This thread seems to continue with how much she would like to regain her daughter's confidence (of course this thread is seen only in hindsight and is only my thread). We have begun to discuss possible signs to her daughter and to herself.

Reflecting Break

I took a few minutes to converse with myself and then rejoined her to share those thoughts.

CONSULTANT: Let me summarize what I heard you say and then you can tell me whether I'm off base or not.

It sounds to me as if you are wondering about all this and perhaps anxious or scared when you have seen other people, friends even, being at the same stage of their life with nothing. Sounds like you are wondering what this means and whether you are going to go the same way. You are wondering what this might mean to your daughter and your relationship with her. It seems that you are angry with your mom and your husband; that they could be right in saying what they do about you.

And while you are wondering about all this and wondering why you turn to drugs when you are stressed, it sounds like you are thinking you would like things to be different and that you are looking for an answer. You are thinking how you would like things to be and one of the ways you would like things to be different is to have your daughter see you differently.

CLIENT: Hmm, hmm.

CONSULTANT: You would like for her to see what you know about yourself, which is that you can be responsible and dependable. You can be on time. You would also like to have a normal structured life with your daughter involved in your life and you in hers.

I guess with all that I am struck by your doing some things recently. I am struck with your moving here (*referring to her mother's insistence that she move here and get into counseling*). Sounds like this was not necessarily your first choice of things to do.

CLIENT: No (*she laughs*).

CONSULTANT: I am struck with how you are putting up with your mother. I cannot imagine how it must be to live with your parent again. I would imagine you must feel like an adolescent again.

If all of this is part of your deciding to make a change for yourself, I would like to honor your putting yourself through all this, living with your mom, putting up with her telling you what to do. I suppose the more positive side is that you are putting yourself in a position where drugs are less accessible. Even last night, you chose to go to bed rather than seeking out some drugs.

I am not sure what all these things mean, if this means you are just thinking about making changes or if you are deciding, "I want to do more about this."

CLIENT: I just know that if anyone can help me get back on my feet it is my mother. She is financially able to help out and I know that she will help me set myself up in an apartment or condo.

I don't know if by going to counseling, a light is going to go on and I will realize, "Oh, I don't need drugs anymore." I don't think that is going to happen.

I am thinking I don't want the same thing to happen all over again and go back to drugs and then have everyone abandon me—saying, "You had your second chance." I don't know. All these things are going through my head.

CONSULTANT: Well, I think it is good to be thinking about all this because you don't want more of the same. Sounds like you want it to be different.

CLIENT: Everyone says, "You can do this if you want to." But I'm thinking, "Am I really going to be able to do this?" In my mind I am wondering how this is going to happen. I am not convinced that I am never going to touch drugs again.

CONSULTANT: Sounds like a lot of things to think about.

I am not sure where you are with this then, if you want to set another appointment. I think it would be good for you to keep thinking about all this. If you do decide you want to come back, I would suggest that you notice any times when you are doing what you want or find yourself resisting the temptation to do drugs. Changes are always unique. You can have ten people go through NA and each one of them will do it differently. So, I would suggest you notice what you do that you like, so that you can build your own way.

CLIENT: I would like to set another appointment. I think it would be good.

SECOND MEETING, ABOUT ONE WEEK LATER

The client came into the office complaining about her mother. Her mother had driven her to the meeting and in the car they began arguing.

CLIENT: She's acting like a full-time babysitter. She watches me all the time. She insists on driving me everywhere. She takes me to every NA meeting and she insists that I go with her to all of her things. If she goes out with her friends, she insists on my going with her. If she goes to a garden meeting, she insists on my going with her. She's a fucking babysitter.

She continues with the story of how her mother is watching her all the time and not letting her alone. She said her mother got all upset the other night. She went to an NA meeting and at the meeting met someone she had talked to before. They decided to go out after the meeting for a while. She said she left the meeting at 10 and when she arrived back at her mother's place at 2, her mother was sitting outside the door. She did not realize that she had her mother's only key to the door and that she had been sitting there all that time. She said that her mother was furious and that she just went into question after question about where she was. She said she could understand how her mother would be mad and how she would be suspicious of what she was doing, but this insistence on knowing what she was doing at all times was driving her nuts. She began to cry as she spoke of how she thought everyone wanted her to fail.

As she talked about her frustration with her mother, I became curious about how she was coping with all this, how she had not decided to just go back home and how she was not doing drugs at a time that was so stressful.

She said that she did not want to return home yet but she had thought of it given how her mother was acting. She had not done drugs in the past week since our last meeting, even though her mother was trying to make her feel so guilty.

CONSULTANT: Sounds like a lot to put up with. In terms of what you came in about last week, not doing drugs, you have not done any?
CLIENT: No.
CONSULTANT: *How have you done that?*

I am curious about how she is managing to resist the drugs given the stress. I am also curious if her managing to resist the drugs could become a story of success.

CLIENT: It's been a miracle.
CONSULTANT: You've thought of it?
CLIENT: Yes, every day.
CONSULTANT: *So, how have you done it?*
CLIENT: The meetings have been helpful. I have gone to all kinds of meetings, NA, AA, CA. I think that it helps to sit around and listen to what other people are saying.

I'm not shocked by what they say, because I realize eventually I would have been there. It is just heart-wrenching what people have done and stooped to. But, they are not doing drugs anymore. They have gone nine months, two years, or something else, and here I am so proud that I have gone 11 days. (*She laughs.*)

But it is not for lack of wanting it. I just wish my mother would let up on the noose.

I am struck by the fact that in the first meeting she talked of her desire to stay off drugs and win back the trust and confidence of her daughter and others. In this meeting she seems to want to talk about her mother, a situation that did not come up in our first conversation. So, I ask which she would rather talk about.

CONSULTANT: So, what would you like to talk about today—not doing coke or the situation with your mom?

CLIENT: I want to get myself strong so that I can go back home, but I cannot cope with her. I want her to relax and back off.

I don't know . . . I don't know what I want from today. How about you telling her to move out for a while and leave me alone?

She appears too upset to talk of options. Instead I want to be affirming and appreciate what she is going through. At the same time I am struck that, despite how angry and frustrated she is with her mother, in part she is empathic with her and obviously cares a great deal about her.

CONSULTANT: I'm impressed that despite all this you can be as understanding of her as you are.

CLIENT: Well, I don't want to go home yet. I want to go back and see my daughter and be strong and be clean. And my mother, she's been there for me before and I love my mom. But I don't want her threats. She says to me, "This is my house and you have to go by my rules or I will just put you on the bus." Who needs that?

She seems to be angry and yet wanting her time here with her mother to work so that she can return home stronger in the direction of her goals. She seems calmer. I attempt to acknowledge what she has said and to inquire how she would like things to be in that relationship.

CONSULTANT: Yeah (*sadly*). So, things have been tough to say the least. I have a pretty good idea of how things have been going; can you say a little of *how you would like things to be going between the two of you?*

CLIENT: I'd like her to treat me as an adult, not hold my hand all over the place.

CONSULTANT: More like an adult. How do you mean?

CLIENT: I don't know, just back off and trust me some (*exasperated*).

CONSULTANT: How do you mean?

CLIENT: If she would trust me with a little money and not get all funny when I want to go out by myself or stay home by myself.

CONSULTANT: This would mean a lot to you.

CLIENT: Well, to say the least, I wouldn't get so pissed off. I mean, I know she has lots of reasons to be suspicious.

CONSULTANT: How do you mean?

CLIENT: I've lied to everybody at some point. So, I know she is wondering what I am up to and what she can believe. But she doesn't know what this is all about. She's reacting like I am some TV character. All she knows about drugs is what she sees in movies or on TV. So, she's acting like some detective or parole officer. She thinks anybody I talk to on the phone must be a dealer or addict.

Many questions are coming to mind at this point. With regard to our "Who wants what?" question, I am curious about whether and what her mother may want at this point. Is her mother a client for change also? At the same time that I am thinking of customership, the client seems to feel that her mother does not really know what is going on and that her mother is basing her actions on some TV stereotype. Does this mean that the client feels misunderstood by her mother? If so, in what way would she like her mother to understand her? What picture of herself would she like her mother to have? What would be signs to her mother of this truer picture of herself?

CONSULTANT: So, it sounds like you are thinking your mother is not just upset but wants some things to be different as well?
CLIENT: Definitely.
CONSULTANT: So, she would like some things different and you would like her to have a truer picture of you, not some movie character.
CLIENT: Yeah, I think she just gets freaked when she does not know where I am. She thinks the worst. I think she wants the same as I do though. I think she wants me to get clean and do the right thing with my daughter.
CONSULTANT: So, you both want the same things.

It was time to take a break. If time had allowed I would have liked to pose some questions in line with the thread of conversation: Given that her mother is interested in change as well, what would be signs to her mother that she, the client, was getting "clean and doing right by her daughter"? If her mother is interested in changes in their relationship, what would be signs to her mother that the relationship was improving? Given that she wants her mother to "back off," what would her mother say would be changes by the client that would make her "back off"? What would she like her mother to know about her or what picture would she like her mother to have of her?

Reflecting Break

CONSULTANT: I am sorry that you are having to go through these arguments with your mother and that she does not know what is really going on with you. She apparently does not know how you are struggling with staying away from the drugs and doing the right thing. I found myself wondering how it would make a difference to her if she knew.

I would like to salute you for staying away from the drugs and for your desire to be recognized as trustworthy and caring about your daughter. I am still wondering how you are managing to stay away from the drugs and how you are managing to keep your mind on what you ultimately want, to be strong and for things to be right between you and your daughter.

CLIENT: I am pleased that I have stayed away from the drugs but I wish my mother would understand that she is just driving me back to them.

THIRD MEETING, ABOUT ONE WEEK LATER

I was concerned that in our scheduling these appointments about one week apart she would not have enough time to recognize her changes. I was also concerned that this scheduling might lead to some expectations of over-dependence upon the consultation. She insisted, however, that her mother would not think she was serious about therapy if she were not coming every week.

When she came in, I asked what if anything was any different or better. She said things were about the same. She said that she was thinking after the last meeting that the main issue is the drugs. She would like other things to be different, like with her mother, but the main thing is the drugs. She didn't know what she was supposed to do, however, because everybody—her mother, her sister, and her husband—were all pushing and pulling.

I asked why, with all this pushing and pulling, she was going along and hadn't gone home. It certainly would make sense to me if she decided that going through all this was not what she wanted or maybe not worth it. Instead she said that she did not want to fail. She said she wanted to stay, get a grasp of the meetings, figure out why she was an addict, and be strong enough to go back with new tools. She stated that she also felt that no one was supporting her, that they all seemed to expect her to fail.

As we talked about that further, she stated that if things were going her way she would continue to be clean and eventually she would be with her daughter. I was curious if her daughter would say that she was still hopeful. She said that by her phone conversations with her she knew that her daughter was looking forward to her coming back. I asked what was it about her that her daughter would say still gave her hope about her.

She said, "I know that she knows that I am a good person and she just wants me to be like I used to."

CONSULTANT: *If she was here now listening in on what we have been talking about, what would she say?*

I am inviting her daughter's reflection at this time. Given that she has been talking about how she wants her daughter to be able to trust her, given the efforts she is making in some difficult circumstances, and given that she is hopeful, I am curious about what her daughter might say about these things. If this were a conjoint meeting, I would ask the daughter directly.

CLIENT: She would be happy that I am coming here, going to meetings and not doing drugs.

CONSULTANT: *How would she say that makes a difference to her?*

CLIENT: She just wants to know that she can count on what I say, that I do not lie to her. She wants to know that if I say I will be back, that I will be back.

CONSULTANT: Would she think you are making progress on that now?

CLIENT: I hope so. That's the way I used to be. I wasn't like this her whole life. When I was pregnant with her, I didn't take anything, no drinks, no drugs for 13 months. I just said to myself, "Well I'm pregnant now."

CONSULTANT: You didn't do any? (*I am struck by the contrast of times when she has been engaging drugs and the times when she didn't.*)

CLIENT: No, I even tried to quit smoking.

CONSULTANT: *How did you do all that?*

CLIENT: I didn't want the baby to be affected. I knew if I drank, I would go to the point of blacking out. They suggested pain pills to me at one point. I asked if that wouldn't affect her. The nurse said to just take a little. I said, "No. I didn't want a baby high on pain pills."

CONSULTANT: How come? (*wanting to acknowledge her integrity and yet inviting her to expand on the emerging story*) Others would have done that and more.

CLIENT: I think that is horrible. (*crying*)

CONSULTANT: Really? (*sadly as well*)

CLIENT: Yes, I can't see how anyone can do that to a baby.

CONSULTANT: (*sadly and yet encouraging*) Good for you. This is what you are wanting for your daughter and for you now. And this is what makes you hopeful you can do this now. You went 13 months without.

Still, you are not pregnant now. How are you doing this?

CLIENT: (*sadly*) I don't know.

Her sadness and her determination to make a difference as a mother touch me. I want to ask her more but we are short on time and I take my break.

Reflecting Break

CONSULTANT: First thing, I was touched by what you said about your daughter—that you think she has hope for you, fears too, that you will do this. It sounds like your sense is that if she were listening in here or watching you lately that she would be pleased and see what you have been doing as indications that her hopes are well founded and that you are doing things to restore her confidence.

So, even if you have not had a lot of contact with her, it sounds like she would see the efforts you are making and be pleased about it. And I think you are doing a lot: putting up with other people's misconceptions about you—not that they do not have reasons for being cautious—and staying here so you'll have the skills to go back and show people you can do it.

It is impressive how you are putting yourself through a lot of frustration and perhaps proving to yourself that you can be counted on.

Last thing, I do not want to seem sentimental about this because this is a very serious and sensitive matter. However, I am very touched by your sense of motherhood and that with your pregnancy you would not even consider substances of any kind. There are things other women have done that you would not even consider a possibility, that even when you were tempted, you did something else.

So, I am impressed with what being a mother means to you in the everyday experience, that you would be putting yourself through all this.

FOURTH MEETING, ABOUT A WEEK AND A HALF LATER

CONSULTANT: Anything any different or better?

CLIENT: Everything is pretty good.

CONSULTANT: Really? (*I am surprised, given the contentious second meeting and the difficulty she spoke of last time.*) How?

CLIENT: Maybe I am getting used to it. Although I did smoke crack last week, and I told my mom. Of course she had a heart attack over it. But ... I am not going to make any excuses over it.

CONSULTANT: You have done it again since then?

CLIENT: Nope, nope. Cause after I did it, I thought, this is defeating the whole purpose of my being here. This is stupid. I might as well go back home and kill myself.

I don't know why I did it. It was so easy to get. So, yes, I did it. But I have been going to some really good meetings and after last week I just haven't wanted to.

I am almost overwhelmed by the events and I want to know more about what she has already said. Given what she said, I am most curious, not about her having done crack, but how she decided to stop. In traditional substance abuse counseling orientations, we would be curious about the triggers or how this relapse occurred. Instead, I am curious about what may have been different. Was it different that she did it only once? Given that she could have continued and not shown up today, I am curious about how she decided to stop. All of these questions flow from the thought that a recurrence of the problem is not necessarily all bad. Something about her stopping may lead to an empowering story creation.

CONSULTANT: *I am still curious about how afterwards you decided not to.*

CLIENT: Because after you do it, you feel like shit. And you wonder, "Why did I do that?"

CONSULTANT: Really?

CLIENT: Back home I would go for two to three days and then I would just crash and sleep and wake up and not feel so bad. But when you go only a couple hours, you feel . . .

I am struck by the difference. Before, she would go for days. How is it this time that she decided to stop? So, I invite her into creating a story of difference and empowerment. The question, "So how did you decide to stop at a couple hours?" implies a deliberate decision on her part. I am curious about how she decided to stop and how that might make a difference to her. While she, like many people, might be focused on the taking of crack, I am curious about how it might make a difference to her to story it differently.

CONSULTANT: *So, how did you decide to stop at a couple hours?*

CLIENT: I just left.

CONSULTANT: That was a deliberate choice?

CLIENT: Oh yeah! I just kept thinking, my mother is going to be all over me. I didn't want to go through all that. But I had to go through all that anyway cause I told my mother when I got back and she went off the wall.

CONSULTANT: You told her?

CLIENT: Yes, I just listened and she went on and on.

CONSULTANT: Was that different how you handled that?

I am curious about how she might have handled this situation differently and how it might have worked out better even if it was unpleasant for her. In the past, she might not have told anyone. Was it different for her to just listen and not defend herself or argue? Was it different even for her to go home as opposed to staying out?

CLIENT: Yes, any other time I would have just walked away and said, "Oh, please!"

CONSULTANT: So, how come you did not do that?

CLIENT: I really don't know. I mean, I don't have any money. But beyond that I don't want to go back yet. I have come down here, my mother is helping me out. If I went back now I'd be the same as when I left. I want to be stronger when I go back.

I am struck by how she is thinking of the consequences and the possibilities and opting for actions that lead to what she wants—to be stronger when she goes back.

I asked her what would be signs to her that she was stronger or strong enough and she said she did not know. However, later she talked about a conversation she had over the phone with her husband. As she talked about the conversation, I asked how or in what way the conversation was different. All she could say was that somehow she was not as defensive, that she knew she was doing some good things.

A little later I asked what would be further signs to her that she was moving in the right direction. She stated that she and her mother have a love-hate relationship. If she were getting along with her mother, that would be a further sign.

I asked if there was anything else that would tell her that things were continuing in the right direction. She said that she had been thinking that her mother had all the control. But lately, she was thinking that her mother was just reacting to what she thought she knew about crack and about her. So, one other good thing was that her mother was going out without her tonight and leaving her alone. This could be a sign of some different thinking on her mother's part, but she did not know how her mother might be thinking differently about her.

Reflecting Break

CONSULTANT: I am almost heady or light-headed for you about this. That is too strong really, but I am happy for you how you are doing these things. Not that I am not scared for you as well. It sounds though like you are less angry about all this and perhaps a bit more satisfied.

I am struck by how you decided to end the smoking at two hours—that you are continuing with your decision to make a difference and return home stronger. I am curious about how your changes might make things different with your mom.

I am glad for you that things are a little different with your mother. I wonder if her going out tonight is a sign of her increased confidence in you or her recognition that she cannot control you and therefore to her this change is really all your responsibility.

So, I just want to continue cheering you on.

FIFTH MEETING, ABOUT TWO WEEKS LATER

The meeting started with her telling me that she had been out of town for a little under a week. She had visited with a girlfriend. I asked if anything of the visit was different. Asking if anything was different or better invites clients to consider that option or possibility even if they were not thinking that way when they came in.

CLIENT: She felt more at ease. She said I looked better and healthier and that I seemed to have a better frame of mind.
CONSULTANT: You think so as well?
CLIENT: Before, when I saw her I was either depressed or I had an "I don't give a fuck" attitude.
CONSULTANT: What makes you think your attitude is different?
CLIENT: Because I am excited that I am getting to start my life over. (*said tentatively*) I don't know . . .

CONSULTANT: I am struck that you feel different.

CLIENT: Before it was so easy. When I did drugs, I didn't care about anything. So, if something was really bothering me, I got this feeling like, "It's not that bad. I'll deal with it later." I think, smoking crack, that was the biggest draw cause I was constantly thinking, "I am so upset. I gotta do something. I gotta get out of here." But I was just like so imprisoned, like there was nothing I could do right. But when I got high, it would seem like everything was not that bad; it will work out in the end. That is so stupid. Nothing gets better if you don't do anything.

It just got worse and worse, the worrying, the crack, the feeling depressed, more drugs.

CONSULTANT: What are you doing now?

CLIENT: I am not doing the drugs and I don't feel so bad, so helpless. It is not such a vicious circle. I am thinking about what I want to do. I don't know how to explain it all yet. I still think about the drugs and getting high, but I am coming to the point where I think, "Just think about how depressed you are going to be afterwards."

She stated that the other difference in her visit was that she did not feel defensive before and during the time she was there. Previously, her friend knew she had been doing drugs. So, she was always guarded with her friend and afraid she would be asking if she was high or her friend would be critical of her. This time she said to herself that it was okay if her friend asked because she was feeling better about doing something about her drug use.

She also said that she had sought out a NA meeting while she was there. I asked how she decided to do that given that her mother was not there to insist.

CLIENT: Even if I don't go every day—when I do go—I feel positive about things. They are so willing to put up with you. You just have to have a real desire to get off drugs.

CONSULTANT: That's different. Others are critical. *How does this NA attitude make a difference for you?*

CLIENT: Mom's attitude is so negative. I don't want to talk to her. In NA they only ask that I don't want to get high. I never had positive reinforcement. I just want to get back into the adult world.

Reflecting Break

CONSULTANT: I am happy for you about some of the things you are doing. I am scared too because there is a part of me that thinks things are going so well and asks what might happen.

I am struck how you are continuing to stay away from the drugs but also how you are thinking differently. It sounds like this change has a lot to do with your thinking of yourself as a mother.

Again, I am happy for you that your visit went well. I am struck how you were more positive about what you are doing and how this made a difference in your relationship with your friend. Instead of being defensive or suspicious of what she might be thinking, you were open and relaxed and I suspect that made a difference in how she was with you.

I am also struck how you decided to seek out some meetings and that you are reflecting on how you can make use of them. It sounds like maybe you are listening in a different way, as you say, "Hearing something each time you go, even though they say the same thing at each meeting." I am especially impressed that you went when you could have blown it all off, given that your mother was not there to know the difference.

How you are beginning to think about your future for yourself and your daughter touch me.

CLIENT: Yes, I realize that I am not cured or anything but it has been so many years of alcohol, prescription drugs and so on. This is the first time I'm thinking that maybe I don't need any chemical in me to get through the day. I said to my mother, I just want to get back into life.

SIXTH MEETING, ABOUT TWO WEEKS LATER

She started this meeting by saying that things had been all right but that her mother was still driving her crazy. Her mother was watching where she was going and checking her phone calls. Her mother got angry with her for making a long distance call during prime hours. She said she just wished her mother would let go of the leash a little, that she hated having to answer to her mother, especially when she would ask so many questions.

She complained how her mother wanted her to be more open with her and yet her mother was not open with her about what was going on in her life.

She said that she would have to go back home fairly soon because of her impending court date for the beginning of her divorce proceedings and child custody hearings.

Reflecting Break

Part of my reflections went like this.

CONSULTANT: It sounds really tough. Putting myself in your shoes, I don't know how you are doing it, actually. With all that is going on, I can imagine that many people would be strongly tempted to get high. Somehow, even with the temptations, you are still staying clear-headed.

I don't know where your mother is with all this or what would make her let go a little. Maybe she has some ideas and perhaps it would be worth it to talk with her about her ideas. If you were a teenager living at home, I would suggest that what could make a difference to a parent is to be more open about what you are thinking, even the temptations that you have. That way parents figure they know a little of what is going on rather than trying to guess or figure it out by being suspicious. I don't know if your mom is thinking about it or if she is just the kind of person who needs time to be convinced. On the other hand, maybe nothing you do will make a difference to her and you will just have to cope with her being the way she is. So, I don't know if it is worth a conversation with her or not.

CLIENT: Hmmm. I don't know either.

SEVENTH MEETING, ABOUT ONE WEEK LATER

I asked what might have been any different or better. She calmly replied that things were about the same. On the one hand, her mother was continuing to question how she was spending her money, but on the other hand her mother was now going out with her friends rather than staying home to watch her. We wondered together then if this was a sign of her mother's trusting her more.

She said that one of the things that was different was her own mixture of reactions to her mother's suspicions and to other family relations. I was confused and I asked if things were actually getting worse between them.

CLIENT: No, no. It is just that when I got high, I just pushed things aside or things were not a problem. Now that I am not getting high, I am feeling all of these things, and wondering about all of these things with my family and I am feeling defensive.

Like when my mother came home last night, I felt defensive with her even though I had not done anything.

CONSULTANT: So, it is hard to know if your mother is just curious, or worried, or on the other hand, if she has already concluded that you were out getting drugs.

So, in spite of all this, you are still staying clear-headed?

CLIENT: Yes, yes. It's getting harder every day. I just keep thinking that I want to be able to go back with a clear head and a clear mind.

CONSULTANT: What makes you want the clear head?

CLIENT: Cause I will be going back home soon and I am going to have to start with everyone up there. They have not seen me in over a couple months and they will be the same as my mother was. My husband is going to be very suspicious. So, I can't do drugs up there.

CONSULTANT: Hmmm. So, what would make him think you were different?

CLIENT: If I didn't disappear for two or three days.

CONSULTANT: He is still interested in your being different?

CLIENT: Oh, yes. He wants me to be different for our daughter. He wants me to be a good mom for our girl.

She stated that her husband too was looking for signs that she was dependable and could be trusted again. Despite the impending divorce, she felt that while he was suspicious, he too wanted her to make the changes.

We discussed for a while her worries about the impending custody hearings. I remembered her saying earlier in the meeting that she was staying clear-minded but that it was very difficult. Then I asked her again about how she was staying clear-headed and clear of crack.

CONSULTANT: So, you're still thinking of it?

CLIENT: Yes, I still dream of it. Every night I have this dream where I go out and buy some. Then I cook it and right about the time I am ready to smoke, I wake up. What a nightmare! What does this mean?

CONSULTANT: That you're frustrated (*laughing*). So, how are you doing something else rather than coke or crack?

CLIENT: Sometimes, I think about what would happen if I got caught.

As the meeting drew to a close, I asked if she thought she was on track, that is, basically doing what she needed to, or did she think she needed to do something more or different. The reason for this question is the assumption that clients may only need possibilities and a sense of agency that they did not think they had before. Agency means the ability to do something. If before clients may have felt they could do nothing to change their situation or that they were helpless, agency is a sense of ability or possibility. So, in this situation, I am curious, given her changes, whether she feels she needs to continue what she is already doing or whether she feels she needs to do something more or different.

CONSULTANT: Recently, you have been talking about wanting to not do the drugs but also to stay clear-headed and become stronger in your skills. Do you think you are basically on track with all that or are you thinking that you need to do something more or different?

CLIENT: When I keep myself thinking of the short term, I think I am doing okay. But when I start thinking longer, I get all into, "What if this happens, or what if that happens?" Then, I don't know what I am thinking.

CONSULTANT: So, it's better to keep your thinking to the short term, one day at a time, given the uncertainties of the court and everything else.

Reflecting Break

CONSULTANT: I think it is just great how you are handling things.

CLIENT: Really? I feel like I could go off the deep end at any moment.

CONSULTANT: Yeah, it sounds very hard. However, with the difficulties, with all these uncertainties about so many things, I am excited how you are still clear about your desire to stay clear-headed and dependable to your daughter and others. All of these things being up in the air would drive me nuts.

CLIENT: This is true. I have always been so structured. I really need to be working or something.

CONSULTANT: Well, I guess you know what it is to not be clear-headed and so you probably know more than I what it means to have clear head.

With regard to the difficulty with your mother, I think that any time that any of us are with our parents, no matter what age, parents do not stop being parents. They ask questions and they still act at times like the parents they were when we were younger. So I am not surprised that you feel defensive sometimes even when you haven't done anything. Sometimes a parent's worry is enough to inspire guilt or defensiveness. It does not necessarily mean anything about you.

At the same time I am happy for you that your mother apparently is seeing something different about you and is backing off and trusting you even more to be home without her.

Keep up what you are doing.

EIGHTH MEETING, ABOUT TWO WEEKS LATER

The meeting opened with a discussion of how things were better with her mother. She said they had a big blow-out last week and since then her mother had been leaving the house even more without her. During that fight and resulting talk she stated to her mother that if she were going to do drugs she would find a way regardless of whether her mother was home or not. She also stated that she had been doing well and that she had recently given her no reason to worry. With that her mother seemed to be showing more faith in her by going out more and doing things she would normally do.

I asked what would be further ways that she would like her mother to be different with her at this time. As we talked about how she would like her mother to show more faith in her, we also talked about how her mother might be enjoying her being with her. With this she began to tear up as she talked about how much it meant to her that her mother was there for her. Earlier when she was younger her mother had been very depressed and not there for her.

As she talked about what else from her mother's point of view would inspire even more confidence, she again said that her mother would probably say that her being more open would inspire more faith. She thought that if she opened up more to her mother, her mother would say she would have more of an understanding. However, she thought that she was just like her, a private person, and therefore not likely to be any more open.

This discussion of being more open led to the following dialogue about how she was not being as defensive and sarcastic with everyone lately.

CONSULTANT: What's different that you are not doing this?
CLIENT: I haven't for a long time been facing things.
CONSULTANT: So, how is it that you are facing things now?
CLIENT: It's just that when you come down from drugs, you are so depressed and you feel so out of control of anything, everything, and so, if anyone expected anything of me, I didn't want to deal with anything.

I never thought, "I am such a drug addict!" I just wanted to be left alone and I was always paranoid of what people wanted or what they were doing.

Now, I don't know, I am just sitting and thinking about how I feel. Now, I ask why are they saying these things to me. They aren't just trying to hurt me or maybe they really don't understand.

CONSULTANT: Sounds like you are giving people the benefit of a doubt.

The meeting concluded with a discussion of whether she thought she was basically on track by pursuing a clear head and being dependable or was she thinking she needed to do something else. She thought she was doing the right things. She had decided to go back home in a week to begin work on the divorce proceedings and custody arrangements.

Reflecting Break

Part of my reflections was the following.

CONSULTANT: I am excited for you that you are returning home and how you are dealing with things, the attorney and your family. It does sound like you are trying to really understand why people are saying things to you or acting suspiciously sometimes. Rather than just reacting with sarcasm or assuming that they don't care, it sounds like you are giving them the benefit of good intentions and trying to understand why they are acting as they are.

I am touched by how important your mother is to you, and how the two of you can be so direct and angry and still recognize how important you are to each other.

FINAL MEETING

In the beginning of this meeting, we talked about how things were okay despite her excitement and anxiety about returning home the next day. She stated that as she had been talking with her husband on the phone, she could hear his skepticism and suspicions about her change. While she was tempted to get defensive, she didn't.

We talked about what fears her family might have.

CLIENT: I don't know why, but that is the farthest thing from my mind. I just want . . . I don't know . . . you know, anyone could ask me to take a drug test and I don't want to even have to worry about that.

CONSULTANT: Sounds like it's not that you don't have a lot of other things to think about.

CLIENT: Yes (*laughing*). But sometimes I think, "Could it be that I'm finally ending my drugs?" Right now, I feel like I am. It is almost scary. But when I think, no more, ever, I go, I don't know. Maybe just one time, one night.

But I know I can't. Probably the longer I go without, the stronger I am. As long as I think I cannot do it even once, I don't have to worry about it.

Reflecting Break

CONSULTANT: Best of luck. I think if I were in your shoes, I'd be on pins and needles. I imagine going home is going to be great and hard—great to see your daughter and hard at the same time. I imagine that people may say and do things based on how they used to know you. They may not see right away what you know about yourself. You have seen yourself make changes every day, but they may react to you as you were when you left. I am worried for you that it may hurt if they do not respond as you would hope.

I hope it all goes great.

The meetings were scheduled about a week or two apart. Because her mother wanted the reassurance that she was working on her problems, she decided it was best to come often. We have no set rules about the frequency of meetings. We usually ask at the end of each meeting whether and when to meet again. Usually, as clients begin to experience a sense of personal agency, they extend the time between meetings. If there had not been the issue of her mother's need for reassurance by regular meetings, we probably would have had fewer or less frequent consultations.

This consultation is a good example of a client's having several preferences for how she wanted her life to be going differently. Some were stated as the absence of some present behavior and others were stated in more positive terms. The absence of doing drugs seemed to provide signs to her in hindsight that she was making changes. The acting clear-headedly and creating trust with her daughter and mother seemed to be a positive indication to her in the present.

Throughout the times I met with her I was always deeply touched by her dedication to her daughter and how much she wanted to show her daughter how she could be responsible.

She reflected to me at the last meeting that our meetings had been very helpful. She appreciated the encouragement and faith.

Conclusion
Ending—But Not Ending

We have suggested a redescription and thus a new language for helping professions and for what we used to call brief therapy. If we abandon the problem/solution distinction and the discourses of pathology and deficit and instead orient ourselves to desire as evolving in conversation, *therapy* must be replaced with some other term. We have chosen to call what we do *personal consultation* and to conceptualize our work as facilitating *conversations* around client preferences and possibilities.

Our proposal to abandon the discourses that are supportive of the word *therapy* is a radical one that cuts to the root and heart of how our professions have defined themselves over the years. We believe that the language of personal consultation opens up possibilities for us to be more respectful of our clients and the diversity of their lives.

We believe this language allows us to see our clients as well intentioned people who want to create something positive in their future. It allows us to be in alignment with them, standing beside them or behind them, and encouraging their creative efforts. Stepping out of the expert or the evaluator position allows us to be interested, curious, and encouraging and to engage in joint exploration of client desires. No longer do we think that there is something wrong with our clients; in fact they are very right for wanting something better in their future.

While this is the ending of this book, this is not an ending. In 1992, we wrote:

> This book like any book is just a narrative of where we are at this point in time. . . . We know that our narrative provides the opportunity for further conversation with the readers and they with us. In light of this

assumption, we hope that this is the beginning of many useful conversations with you. (p. 259)

Our first book did indeed lead to enjoyable, enlightening, and useful conversations with readers and clients. We hope that this one leads to even more conversations for us with you and for you and your clients.

References

American Psychiatric Association. (1994). *Diagnostic and statistical manual of mental disorders* (4th ed.). Washington, DC: Author.

Andersen, T. (1987). The reflecting team: Dialogue and metadialogue in clinical work. *Family Process, 26,* 415–428.

Andersen, T. (1991). Guidelines for practice. In T. Andersen (Ed.), *The reflecting team: Dialogues and dialogues about the dialogues.* New York: Norton.

Anderson, H. (1997). *Conversation, language, and possibilities.* New York: Basic Books.

Anderson, H., & Goolishian, H. (1984). Problem-determined systems: Towards a transformation in family therapy. *Journal of Strategic and Systemic Therapies, 5*(4), 1–13.

Anderson, H., & Goolishian, H. (1988). Human systems as linguistic systems: Preliminary and evolving ideas about the implications of clinical theory. *Family Process, 27,* 371–394.

Bandler, R., & Grinder, J. (1979). *Frogs into princes.* Moab, UT: Real People Press.

Barthes, R. (1974). *S/Z.* New York: Hill & Wang.

Beck, A. (1976). *Cognitive therapy and the emotional disorders.* New York: International Universities Press.

Bruner, E. M. (1986). Ethnography as narrative. In V. W. Turner & E. M. Bruner (Eds.), *The anthropology of experience* (pp. 3–20). Chicago: University of Illinois Press.

Bruner, J. (1986). *Actual minds/possible worlds.* Cambridge, MA: Harvard University Press.

Bruner, J. (1990). *Acts of meaning*. Cambridge, MA: Harvard University Press.

Bruner, J. (1991). The narrative construction of reality. *Critical Inquiry, 18*, 1–21.

Buzan, T. (1974). *Using both sides of your brain*. New York: Dutton.

Cecchin, G. (1987). Hypothesizing, circularity, and neutrality revisited: An invitation to curiosity. *Family Process, 26*, 405–413.

Derrida, J. (1978). *Writing and difference* (Alan Bass, Trans.). Chicago: University of Chicago Press.

de Shazer, S. (1985). *Keys to solution in brief therapy*. New York: Norton.

de Shazer, S. (1988). *Clues: Investigating solutions in brief therapy*. New York: Norton.

de Shazer, S., Berg, I., Lipchik, E., Nunnally, E., Molnar, A., Gingerich, W., & Weiner-Davis, M. (1986). Brief therapy: Focused solution-development. *Family Process, 25*, 207–222.

de Shazer, S., & Molnar, A. (1984). Four useful interventions in brief therapy. *Journal of Marital and Family Therapy, 10*(3), 297–304.

Dorfman, R. (Ed.). *Paradigms of clinical social work* (Vol. 2). New York: Brunner/Mazel.

Ellis, A. (1962). *Reason and emotion in psychotherapy*. Secaucus, NJ: Lyle Stuart.

Epston, D., & Roth, S. (1994). *Framework for a White/Epston type interview*. Workshop handout.

Eron, J., & Lund, T. (1996). *Narrative solutions in brief therapy*. New York: Guilford.

Foucault, M. (1976). Two lectures. In M. Kelly (Ed.), *Critique and power: Recasting the Foucault /Habermas debate*. Cambridge, MA: MIT Press.

Foucault, M. (1980). *Power/ knowledge: Selected interviews and other writings, 1972–1977*. New York: Pantheon.

Freedman, J., & Combs, G. (1996). *Narrative therapy*. New York: Norton.

Geertz, C. (1983). *Local knowledge: Further essays in interpretive anthropology*. New York: Basic Books.

Gergen, K. J. (1982). *Toward a transformation in social psychology*. New York: Springer-Verlag.

Gergen, K. J. (1985). The social constructionist movement in modern psychology. *American Psychologist, 40*, 266–275.

Gergen, K. J. (1994). *Realities and relationships: Soundings in social constructionism*. Cambridge, MA: Harvard University Press.

Goodman, N. (1978). *Ways of worldmaking*. New York: Hackett.

Griffith, J. L., & Griffith, M. E. (1994). *The body speaks: Therapeutic dialogues for mind-body problems*. New York: Basic Books.

Haley, J. (1976). *Problem-solving therapy: New strategies for effective family therapy*. San Francisco: Jossey-Bass.

Haley, J. (1980). *Leaving home*. New York: McGraw-Hill.

Hall, D. (1994). *Richard Rorty: Prophet and poet of the new pragmatism.* Albany: State University of New York Press.

Harr , R. (1979). *Social being: A theory of social psychology.* Oxford: Basil Blackwell.

Harr , R. (1983). *Personal being: A theory for individual psychology.* Oxford: Basil Blackwell.

Hoffman, L. (1983). Diagnosis and assessment in family therapy: II. A co-evolutionary framework for systemic family therapy. *Family Therapy Collections, 4,* 35–61.

Hoffman, L. (1985) Beyond power and control: Toward a "second order" family systems therapy. *Family Systems Medicine, 3,* 381–396.

Hoffman, L. (1993) *Exchanging voices.* London: Karnac.

Lyotard, J. F. (1984). *The postmodern condition: A report on knowledge.* Minneapolis: University of Minnesota Press. (Originally published as *La condition postmoderne: rapport sur le savoir,* 1979, Les Editions di Minuit)

Madanes, C. (1981). *Strategic family therapy.* San Francisco: Jossey-Bass.

Maturana, H. R. (1978). Biology of language: Epistemology of reality. In G. Miller & E. Leneberg (Eds.), *Psychology and biology of language and thought* (pp. 27–63). New York: Academic.

Maturana, H., & Varela, F. (1987). *The tree of knowledge.* Boston: New Science Library.

Mead, G. H. (1910). Social consciousness and the consciousness of meaning. *Psychological Bulletin, VII,* 397–405. (Reprinted in J. Reck [Ed.], *Selected writings of George Herbert Mead.* New York: Bobbs-Merrill, 1964, pp. 123–133.)

Mead, G. H. (1913). The social self. *Journal of Philosophy, Psychology, and Scientific Methods, X,* 374–380. (Reprinted in J. Reck [Ed.], *Selected writings of George Herbert Mead,* pp. 142–149.)

Miller, S., Duncan, B., & Hubble, M. (1997). *Escape from Babel: Toward a unifying language for psychotherapy practice.* New York: Norton.

Miller, S., Hubble, M., & Duncan, B. (Eds.). (1996). *The handbook of solution-focused brief therapy.* San Francisco: Jossey-Bass.

Minuchin, S. (1978). *Families and family therapy.* Cambridge, MA: Harvard University Press.

Nylund, D., & Corsiglia, V. (1994). Becoming solution-forced in brief therapy: Remembering something that we already knew. *Journal of Strategic and Systemic Therapies, 13*(1), 5–12.

O'Hanlon, W., & Weiner-Davis, M. (1989). *In search of solutions: A new direction in psychotherapy.* New York: Norton.

Parry, A., & Doan, R. (1994). *Story re-visions: Narrative therapy in the postmodern world.* New York: Guilford.

Peller, J., & Walter, J. (1998). Solution-focused brief therapy. In R. Dorfman (Ed.), *Paradigms of clinical social work* (Vol. 2) (pp. 71–92). New York: Brunner/Mazel.

Polkinghorne, D. (1988). *Narrative knowing and the human sciences.* Albany: State University of New York Press.

Polkinghorne, D. (1991). Two conflicting calls for methodological reform. *Counseling Psychologist, 19,* 103–114.

Rapp, C. (1998). *The strengths model: Case management with people suffering from severe and persistent mental illness.* New York: Oxford University Press.

Rorty, R. (1979). *Philosophy and the mirror of nature.* Princeton, NJ: Princeton University Press.

Rorty, R. (1982). *Consequences of pragmatism.* Minneapolis: University of Minnesota Press.

Rorty, R. (1989). *Contingency, irony, and solidarity.* Cambridge, England: Cambridge University Press.

Saleebey, D. (Ed.). (1992). *The strengths perspective in social work practice.* New York: Longman.

Sarbin, T. R. (1986). Emotion and act: Roles and rhetoric. In R. Harr (Ed.), *The social construction of emotions* (pp. 83–89). Oxford: Basil Blackwell.

Selvini-Palazzoli, M., Boscolo, L., Cecchin, G., & Prata, G. (1978). *Paradox and counterparadox: A new model in the therapy of the family in schizophrenic transaction.* New York: Jason Aronson.

Shotter, J. (1984). *Social accountability and selfhood.* Oxford: Blackwell.

Shotter, J. (1993). *Conversational realities: Constructing life through language.* London: Sage.

Shotter, J. (1994). Making sense on the boundaries: On moving between philosophy and psychotherapy. In A. P. Griffiths (Ed.), *Philosophy, psychiatry, and psychology* (pp. 55–72) Cambridge, England: Cambridge University Press.

Shotter, J. (1995). In conversation: Joint action, shared intentionality and ethics. *Theory and Psychology, 5,* 49–73.

Speer, D. C. (1970). Family systems: morphostasis and morphogenesis, or Is homeostasis enough? *Family Process, 9,* 259–278.

Taylor, C. (1989). *Sources of the self: The making of the modern identity.* Cambridge, MA: Harvard University Press.

Tomm, K. (1995). *Internalized other interviewing: A sequence for couples work.* Workshop handout.

von Foerster, H. (1982). *Observing systems.* Seaside, CA: Intersystems.

von Foerster, H. (1984). On constructing a reality. In P. Watzlawick (Ed.), *The invented reality: How do we know what we believe we know? Contributions to constructivism* (pp. 41–61). New York: Norton.

von Glasersfeld, E. (1984). An introduction to radical constructivism. In P. Watzlawick (Ed.), *The invented reality: How do we know what we believe we know? Contributions to constructivism* (pp. 17–40). New York: Norton.

von Glasersfeld, E. (1987). The control of perception and the construction of reality. *Dialectica, 33,* 37–50.

References

Wachterhauser, B. (1986). Introduction: History and language in understanding. In B. Wachterhauser (Ed.), *Hermeneutics and modern philosophy.* Albany: State University of New York Press.

Walter, J. (1989). Not individual, not family. *Journal of Strategic and Systemic Therapies, 8*(1), 70–77.

Walter, J. (1997). *Working with the mandated client: A solution-focused interview with John Walter.* Los Angeles: Master'sWork Video Productions.

Walter, J., & Peller, J. (1992). *Becoming solution-focused in brief therapy.* New York: Brunner/Mazel.

Walter, J., & Peller, J. (1996). Rethinking our assumptions: Assuming anew in a postmodern world. In S. Miller, M. Hubble, & B. Duncan (Eds.), *The handbook of solution-focused brief therapy* (pp. 9–26). San Francisco: Jossey-Bass.

Watzlawick, P. (1976). *How real is real?* New York: Vintage.

Watzlawick, P., Weakland, J., & Fisch, R. (1974). *Change: Principles of problem formation and problem resolution.* New York: Norton.

Watzlawick, P. (Ed.). (1984). *The invented reality: How do we know what we believe we know? Contributions to constructivism.* New York: Norton.

Weakland, J., Fisch, R., Watzlawick, P., & Bodin, A. (1974). Brief therapy: Focused problem resolution. *Family Process, 13,* 41–68.

Weiner-Davis, M., de Shazer, S., & Gingerich, W. (1987) Building on pretreatment change to construct the therapeutic solution: An exploratory study. *Journal of Marital and Family Therapy, 13*(4), 359–363.

White, M. (1991). Deconstruction and therapy. *Dulwich Centre Newsletter, 3,* 21–40.

White, M., & Epston, D. (1990). *Narrative means to therapeutic ends.* New York: Norton.

Wittgenstein, L. (1968). *Philosophical investigations* (3rd ed.). (G. & M. Anscombe, Trans.) New York: Macmillan.

Zimmerman, J., & Dickerson, V. (1996) *If problems talked: Narrative therapy in action.* New York: Guilford.

Index